VEGAN Dessert Cookbook

VEGAN Dessert Cookbook

Recipes for
Cakes, Cookies, Puddings, Candies, and More

ALLY LAZARE

PHOTOGRAPHY BY ANNIE MARTIN

ROCKRIDGE PRESS

For general information on our other products and services or to obtain technical support, please contact our Customer Care Department within the United States at (866) 744-2665, or outside the United States at (510) 253-0500.

Rockridge Press publishes its books in a variety of electronic and print formats. Some content that appears in print may not be available in electronic books, and vice versa.

Interior and Cover Designer: Jay Dea
Art Producer: Sue Bischofberger
Editor: Gleni Bartels
Production Editor: Ashley Polikoff
Photography © 2020 Annie Martin
Food styling by Oscar Molinar

ISBN: Print 978-1-64739-523-0
eBook 978-1-64739-524-7
R0

For Audrey and Autumn—

my favorite little bakers in the
whole wide world.

And for Aaron—

because none of this is
possible without you.

Contents

Introduction

Hello, and welcome to the *Vegan Dessert Cookbook*! I'm excited to create all kinds of delicious plant-based desserts with you. I come from a long line of bakers, both home-based and commercial, and I've always said that dessert is a part of my DNA, so writing this book—and sharing it with you—has been a dream come true for me. The kitchen is my playground, and I've always felt most comfortable when surrounded by mixing bowls, spatulas, and flour-dusted surfaces. Nothing brightens my day more than whipping up a fabulous dessert—and sharing it with those I love. This is the feeling I hope you'll experience when using this cookbook.

Almost a decade ago, my little family and I turned to a plant-based lifestyle. I'd gone through major phases of vegetarianism since I was a teenager and was perfectly comfortable not consuming meat products. In 2010, we discovered that our one-year-old daughter had an allergy to dairy, which meant that traditional baking ingredients needed to be replaced with plant-based alternatives. So we embraced a dairy-free and eggless kitchen.

Transitioning to a fully plant-based lifestyle meant learning how to re-create all my favorite desserts without using dairy or eggs. It was a bit of a learning curve, but now that I've done all that legwork, it's time to share what I've learned with you—which is that you can make all your favorite desserts without relying on traditional dairy or egg ingredients and they will still be delicious.

Whether you choose vegan dessert recipes because of dairy or egg allergies, a dedication to a vegan lifestyle, or because it's more convenient, this book has something for everyone. Did you know that vegan baking staples are very pantry-friendly and often have a much longer shelf life than traditional dairy? This is very handy if you're like me and often wander into the kitchen to bake at a moment's notice.

Unlike many vegan dessert cookbooks, this one isn't all about baking. Yes, there are chapters dedicated to cookies and cakes, but there are also delicious recipes for other desserts, like creamy custards, delicious puddings, classic pies, and even frozen and no-bake treats. I've broken the book down by dessert type and included recipes that appeal to bakers of all levels. Most recipes offer homemade and store-bought options for some ingredients, so even if you're a novice in the kitchen or just short on time, you can still make professional-looking desserts. And if you're looking for a dessert for a specific event or occasion, there's a "Desserts by Occasion" index on page 117 to help you find the best dish for your next birthday party, bake sale, or holiday gathering.

I hope this book inspires you to get in the kitchen and start creating fabulous desserts.

Enjoy! . . . .

SETTING UP FOR SWEET SUCCESS

Throughout this book, I'll share recipes and tips for creating delicious desserts that work for plant-based eaters, those with dairy or egg allergies, or anyone who is looking to add a little more plant-based goodness to their diet.

This chapter will focus on the ingredients, tools, and techniques that I love and that you'll need for the recipes in this book. I'll also answer common questions about setting up a vegan pantry, what to use as substitutes for dairy and eggs, and how to adapt recipes for other allergens or intolerances, like gluten or nuts.

Lemon Squares, page 33

ESSENTIAL INGREDIENTS

Let's talk ingredients! Learning how to substitute traditional ingredients with plant-based ones is quite easy once you get the hang of it. And even though there may be a few things in this section that are new to you, you likely already have most in your kitchen.

Fats and Oils

Fats and oils are used to help cream ingredients together, improve structure, and add moisture and tenderness to baked goods. Keep in mind that all oils contain high levels of fat and should be used sparingly. To avoid or cut down on the amount of oil, look to ripe bananas or unsweetened applesauce instead.

Avocados: Avocados can replace butter or oil in a dish and have the added benefit of vitamins, minerals, and "good fats." If you're swapping out butter or oil for avocado, use a 1:1 ratio and adjust your baking temperature and time. For cakes and cupcakes, you'll want to bake at 25°F lower than the recipe states and for a bit longer.

Canola oil: For most recipes that call for oil, I choose canola oil. It's a very neutral oil and won't impart flavor into your dish, like olive oil can, and it's lower in saturated fat than coconut oil.

Coconut oil: Coconut oil has grown in popularity and is often used as a replacement for traditional vegetable or canola oil. It pairs well with chocolate and is good to have on hand for adding a smooth and shiny texture to melted chocolate.

Vegan butter (or margarine): Butter replacements are a quick and easy substitute for traditional butter, and can be used in the same ratio as regular butter. My favorite brand is Earth Balance, but both Country Crock and I Can't Believe It's Not Butter! make plant-based versions that are easily accessible and provide delicious results.

Vegetable shortening: Shortening is a great go-to for pie and tart crusts. Because shortening is a solid fat, it adds more air to batters when combined, giving dishes a fluffier, lighter result. For a tender, flaky piecrust, opt for vegetable shortening instead of oil.

Flavorings and Extracts

Extracts and other flavorings can enhance the flavors of your desserts. Try to choose natural or pure versions when possible, since artificial ones are mostly made from liquid sugars and add sweetness but not flavor.

Almond extract: Using almond extract in almond-based desserts helps boost the nutty flavor. Choose a natural extract if possible and use it sparingly. It's very strong (especially artificial extract), and too much can be unpleasant.

Citrus zest: The fastest way to brighten any baked good is to add the zest of a citrus fruit, whether lemon, lime, or orange. It's fantastic in pie fillings, jams, purees, glazes, and batters.

Cocoa powder: The dried chocolate liquor from a cocoa bean that has had the cocoa butter removed, cocoa powder is always vegan. I prefer Dutch-process cocoa powder since it has a milder, neutral taste. Natural cocoa powder can be more acidic and slightly bitter.

Coffee: Coffee is an amazing way to elevate chocolate desserts. A tablespoon of instant coffee or espresso powder adds richness and depth.

Fruit jams and purees: These are great ways to add natural fruit flavor to fillings and frostings. Because of their sturdy structure, jams work best as fillings. Purees are lighter and thinner, with the seeds already strained out, so they can be used to add flavor (and color).

Spices: Ground cinnamon, nutmeg, ginger, clove, and allspice are also known as "pumpkin spice mix" or "gingerbread mix," and when combined, they are a dessert powerhouse.

Vanilla extract: Vanilla brightens and enhances the flavors of any dessert—even chocolate ones. Splurge on good-quality natural vanilla extract—it's worth it. Artificial vanilla is extremely sweet and can overpower a dessert with a candy-like taste.

Flours, Thickeners, and Binders

Flour and binders are the backbone of desserts, providing the structure that keeps them together. Thickeners prevent fillings and sauces from being too runny or lumpy. Overall, these ingredients give your desserts shape, stability, and great texture.

All-purpose flour: The majority of recipes in this book call for all-purpose flour. When possible, I've included gluten-free substitutes, but generally for the best results, I recommend using all-purpose. If gluten isn't an issue, but you want to move away from white flour, light spelt or light whole-wheat flour can be used instead.

Applesauce: Applesauce both thickens and binds. Choose unsweetened apple-sauce so you don't add extra sugar or sweetness to your dessert.

Aquafaba: The juice (or brine) from chickpeas (or any canned bean, really) has the same properties as an egg white and is a game-changer for making vegan versions of egg white–based desserts. In its raw form (straight from the can), it can be used to replace eggs in baking. To replace a whole egg, use 3 tablespoons of aquafaba. To replace just an egg white, use 2 tablespoons.

Bananas: Bananas are a great substitute for eggs. They help bind ingredients—a great use for overripe ones sitting on your counter! As a general rule, one mashed banana is equal to one egg when baking.

Egg replacers: Powdered egg replacers, which are commonly made from both potato and tapioca starches and baking soda, are an easy way to replace eggs in vegan baking. They usually involve mixing a small quantity with water and letting the mixture thicken before adding it to your wet ingredients. Each one is a little different, so always follow package directions.

Flaxseed: Flaxseed is incredibly good for you. It provides healthy fats, anti-oxidants, and fiber to any dish. Ground flaxseed mixed with water forms a paste known as a "flax egg" and is a natural, easy substitute for eggs in baking. Typically 1 tablespoon of ground flaxseed mixed with 2 tablespoons of hot water is equivalent to one large egg.

Elevate Your Basics

Using fruits, nuts, spices, and other flavorings is a great way to add deliciousness to your desserts, but learning a few simple tricks to elevate those basics can boost your desserts to another level and broaden your baking horizons. For example:

Toasting: Just a couple of minutes in a dry pan on the stove or on a rimmed baking sheet in the oven helps release a nut's oils and intensify its flavor. In the same way, toasting shredded coconut allows the natural sugars to caramelize, giving it incredible flavor.

Reading your labels: When shopping at the store, be sure to read ingredient lists. In general, the fewer ingredients the better. It's also best if you can recognize the names of the ingredients as actual food items (i.e., the fewer chemical-sounding terms the better), which typically means that item is less processed. For example, if you're making a dessert that calls for pumpkin, grab the pumpkin puree, not the pumpkin pie filling. Natural fillings let you control the amount of sugar and give you more authentic fruit flavor instead of just sugary sweetness.

Fresh vs. frozen: Fresh fruit's always a great choice when in season, but if you're craving a peach cobbler in the dead of winter, don't hesitate to reach for a bag of frozen fruit. Frozen fruits are picked at the height of harvest and flash-frozen at their peak, so they're always ready to go. For best results, defrost your fruit first and drain any excess water before using in a recipe.

Powdered sugar: Also known as icing sugar or confectioners' sugar, this very light, powdery sugar is fantastic for thickening and stabilizing glazes and frostings.

Rolled oats: Whole or ground oats naturally absorb liquid, so they're great for thickening and binding baked goods. Oats have a lower glycemic index than processed white flour and are healthier because they contain the whole grain. They also add a nutty flavor when baked.

Dairy Alternatives

"Dairy" is an essential component to dessert-making because it's often the main source of liquid that helps combine dry ingredients. It's also used to add flavor, soften textures, and give baked goods their golden-brown color.

Canned coconut milk: Like other alternative milks, canned coconut milk is a great substitute for traditional dairy. Choose full-fat over light versions since the fat helps thicken and stabilize desserts. Coconut milk is also excellent for making homemade vegan whipped cream.

Coconut cream: Coconut cream is the thick, solid, creamy part of coconut milk that you often find at the top of the can. You can now buy entire cans of just coconut cream, which works quite well for recipes that call for heavy cream or whipped cream. As with coconut milk, coconut cream is also an excellent base for homemade whipped cream topping.

Coconut yogurt: Coconut yogurt is great as a substitute for traditional yogurt or as a lower-calorie replacement for sour cream or whipped cream in recipes.

Plant-based milks: Plant-based milk can be used as a substitute for traditional milk in any recipe. As a general rule, I stick to plain, unsweetened milks because they don't add sugar or flavors. Unsweetened almond milk is my go-to, but if you're avoiding nuts, unsweetened soy milk works just as well.

Soy cream: Soy cream is a soy-based heavy cream. Belsoy makes one that is specifically for cooking and baking. Silk makes an alternative creamer typically used in coffee but that works well for baking too. Soy cream is much thicker than soy milk. I typically use coconut cream in my recipes, but you can use soy cream as well.

Vegan cream cheese: Vegan cheese has grown in popularity, making it readily available in most grocery stores. When making cream cheese–based desserts, I prefer Daiya or Tofutti brands because of their similar consistency to traditional cream cheese and their tangy yet neutral flavor.

Sugars and Sweeteners

Agave nectar: Agave nectar is a plant-based sweetener often used to replace honey because of its golden sheen, stickiness, and sweet but neutral taste. Low on the glycemic index, it's often recommended for diabetic or low-sugar baking. Because agave is naturally sweeter than granulated sugar or honey, you can use less of it and still achieve the same sweet results.

Applesauce: Applesauce works as both a binder and a sweetener in baked goods. Unsweetened applesauce is typically made from apples and water and has no added sugar but is still sweet enough to use as an alternative to granulated sugar. It also has the added benefit of being high in both fiber and vitamin C.

Brown rice syrup: Brown rice syrup has an almost nutty flavor and can be used as an alternative to maple syrup or other liquid sugars. It also works well as a substitute in recipes that require marshmallows as a binder.

Dates: Dates are fantastic, nutritious, natural sweeteners, containing antioxidants, calcium, potassium, and vitamin A. The most common dates used in desserts are Medjool dates, which are soft and chewy and have a caramel-like flavor.

Maple syrup: Maple syrup is a fantastic way to sweeten desserts and add a delicious, caramelized flavor to your dish. Choose 100% Grade A maple syrup for baking, rather than "pancake syrup," which is made from corn syrup and artificial maple extract.

Traditional sugars: I use granulated cane, brown, and raw sugars for different things. For most standard recipes that require a sweetener, such as cakes, I find granulated cane sugar's neutral flavor and color work best. For cookies, bars, or desserts with cinnamon or nuts, I opt for brown sugar, since it has a rich, deep flavor that is both nutty and caramel-like when baked. Brown sugar comes in different varieties, from light to dark, which indicate how much molasses has been added. Raw sugar, such as coconut sugar, is much less refined than granular sugar and contains minor amounts of nutrients. It's also less sweet.

Other Ingredients

These items add texture and flavor to desserts or are premade or store-bought versions of some staple ingredients to save you time in the kitchen without altering flavor or composition.

Boxed cake mixes: Boxed cake mixes offer variety and ease of use—especially to novice bakers—and are a great base for building other, more complicated desserts. Many brands, such as Duncan Hines, Betty Crocker, and Great Value (Walmart's private-label brand), have varieties that are vegan. A quick web search can uncover which flavors are safe for vegan or dairy-free baking.

Instant pudding: Spoon-dessert lovers, rejoice! Many flavors of instant pudding mix are vegan if you use plant-based milk when mixing, including Jell-O brand vanilla, chocolate, banana, lemon, and pistachio. Instant puddings are great to use as fillings for layer cakes and help elevate desserts like trifles.

Nuts: Unless you have an allergy, using almonds, peanuts, pecans, and walnuts is a great way to add flavor, texture, and protein to your desserts.

Premade pie shells: Often found in the frozen section of your grocery store, premade pie and tart shells are a great time-saver and virtually guarantee a perfectly baked crust every time. Look for shells made with vegetable shortening instead of butter and keep one or two on hand in your freezer for "pie emergencies"!

But I Can't Eat This!

You probably already know that vegan desserts offer delicious alternatives to plant-based eaters and people with dairy or egg allergies, but what if you're also concerned about other dietary restrictions such as nut allergies or intolerances to gluten or soy?

Well, you're in luck! Most of the recipes in this book can be adapted to address many common dietary restrictions, and I've included some common substitutions or adaptations in the recipes themselves. As much as possible, I'll list "plant-based milk" as an ingredient, rather than specify a particular type, and let you choose which plant-based option is appropriate for your own dietary restrictions or preferences.

I use nut butters frequently in this book, particularly in the no-bake desserts section. For bakers with nut allergies, I recommend replacing nut-based butters with either a nut-less butter (WOWBUTTER and SunButter are two of my favorites that I've used extensively) or tahini (sesame seed paste) for a more natural alternative. All of these options work well in place of nut butters to add flavor, texture, and binding to each dessert.

Recipes in this book that call for all-purpose flour can be adapted for gluten-free baking by using a 1:1 all-purpose gluten-free flour ratio. I prefer Pillsbury or Bob's Red Mill gluten-free flours, but feel free to choose what works best for you.

Soy is a common replacement for dairy-based products, such as yogurt or cream cheese. For soy allergies or intolerances, I recommend using Daiya brand cream cheese, which is soy-free, or choosing coconut-based products where necessary.

Above all, for any packaged or premade ingredients mentioned in this book, always be sure to read ingredient labels carefully and choose the appropriate replacement based on your individual dietary needs.

Premade puff pastry: Some things are easier bought than made, and if you're short on time or new to baking, premade puff pastry is definitely worth having on hand. Many grocery-store brands are made with vegetable shortening instead of butter, making them an excellent choice for dairy-free bakers.

Shredded coconut: Coconut is another great way to add flavor and texture to bars, cakes, frostings, and other desserts. Desiccated coconut, which refers to fresh coconut that has been dried and shredded or flaked, is most common and is available in both sweetened and unsweetened varieties. I recommend using unsweetened coconut for baking for a more natural flavor.

Store-bought frosting: Store-bought frostings and icings can be real time-savers when it comes to making desserts. Many varieties of Duncan Hines and Betty Crocker frostings are vegan, making them an optimal choice when you can't make your own. Just be aware they're likely much sweeter than homemade versions.

TOOLS AND EQUIPMENT

I wrote this book with the home cook in mind, focusing on recipes that don't require much specialized equipment. You probably already have most of these in your kitchen!

Baking pans and dishes: I recommend having two 9-inch cake pans for layer cakes; one 8-by-8-inch and one 9-by-13-inch baking pan for bars; and a glass or aluminum 9-inch pie dish. I prefer a glass pie dish since you can see the crust as it's baking.

Cookie scoops: These are handy for scooping out equal amounts of batter or dough. I recommend using them for cookies and any dessert baked in a muffin tin. If you don't have cookie scoops, you can use tablespoons. Here is a quick conversion chart for the cookie scoops I list in the book:

1-inch cookie scoop	2-inch cookie scoop	2½-inch cookie scoop
=	=	=
1½ tablespoons	3 tablespoons	4 tablespoons

Electric mixer: Whether it's a stand mixer with whisk and paddle attachments or a small handheld version, electric mixers are great for creaming dry and wet ingredients or whipping wet ingredients into thick fillings or toppings.

Food processor: Food processors are handy for pulsing dry ingredients like nuts and cookies and wet ingredients like dates. If you don't have a food processor, you can crush most dry ingredients in a resealable bag with a rolling pin, and wet items can be processed in a blender.

Measuring glasses, cups, and spoons: I recommend a 2- to 4-cup glass measuring cup for liquids, a set of standard measuring cups for dry ingredients, and standard measuring spoons for both wet and dry ingredients.

Muffin tin: You'll need at least one standard-size 12-cup muffin tin. Having two is ideal for doubling recipes or for recipes that yield more than a dozen.

Piping bags and tips: I recommend both round- and star-point tips in medium and large sizes for easy decorating. Alternatively, a resealable bag with the corner snipped off is a great way to make a piping bag in a pinch!

Rimmed baking sheets: I recommend two 18-by-13-inch sheet pans (half) and three 13-by-9-inch sheet pans (quarter). From baking cookies to catching dripping glazes, these pans have many uses.

Rolling pin: I prefer a 20-inch French-tapered rolling pin for its ease of use, but a standard 12-inch wood or silicone rolling pin works too.

Spatulas and whisks: Rubber spatulas and whisks are great for stirring, mixing, whisking, and combining ingredients, and a metal spatula helps lift baked goods from trays. Offset spatulas (long, narrow tools with blunt, flat blades) make spreading frosting or batter easier. I recommend having a large and a small version.

Wire cooling rack: Allowing air to circulate beneath desserts helps them cool faster. If you have the space, choose a large rack that can accommodate at least 24 cookies.

What Could Go Wrong?

So many factors can influence how a dessert turns out, from the ingredients to the equipment to the weather. Even the most tried-and-true recipe will burn sometimes, and even the most experienced cook can have a "baking fail." Here are a few common dessert-related issues and my troubleshooting advice.

I followed the temperature and timing instructions, but my cookies were burned on the bottom.
Temperatures and times are guidelines only since ovens vary in heat and design. My oven runs hot, so I bake my cookies at 25°F lower than the recipe states and add a few extra minutes if needed. If the outsides of your cookies are baking faster than the insides, try lowering your temp and using the top rack so the cookies are farther away from direct heat.

My cupcakes didn't rise evenly and sunk in the middle.
Baked goods like cakes and cupcakes require a leavening agent, such as baking powder or baking soda, in order to rise. An incorrect amount can cause your cupcakes to deflate, so always be sure to measure exactly using a measuring spoon, since the spoons we eat with are not equal to measuring spoons. Make sure to check the dates on your leavening agents too. Expired ingredients won't react as much as fresh ones.

My buttercream is lumpy or grainy. Why?
Make sure to beat the butter and sugar for as long as the recipe dictates, usually at least 5 minutes. And be sure to use room-temperature butter, since cold butter won't mix evenly and will leave lumps.

TECHNIQUES AND PREPARATION TIPS

While there are inherent differences in vegan ingredients, most of the techniques and tips for creating them are similar to their non-vegan counterparts and should be familiar to most and easy to learn for absolute beginners.

Room temperature is key. Unless specifically stated, bringing ingredients like butter and cream cheese to room temperature before using them is important. If too cold, they won't mix properly, leaving you with grainy frostings or fillings.

Zest first, juice later. Adding both the zest and juice of citrus fruits is a great way to boost the flavor, but you should always zest first and then squeeze out the juice. The firmness of the full fruit makes it easier to shave off the zest.

Just chill! Proper cooling time is essential. Always let desserts cool completely before stacking or frosting. Residual heat can turn your buttercream into a butter pool! No-bake desserts often rely on refrigeration or freezing to hold together, so adhere to the amount of time in the recipe for the best results.

Folding vs. stirring. Delicate ingredients, like buttercream and meringue, need special care when mixing to keep them from deflating or falling apart. Always use a rubber spatula and gently fold them by hand into batters rather than stirring or mixing with an electric mixer. Heavy-handed mixing pushes air out, causing them to deflate and lose their structure. To fold, gently run a spatula down the middle of the bowl and lift over at a slow pace to ensure you're keeping the air in the dish.

Conquer chocolate. Never melt chocolate over direct heat; instead, set up a double-boiler (a heat-proof glass bowl set on top of a pot of simmering water). Put the chocolate in the bowl, and let the indirect heat from the steam gently melt the chocolate. To microwave, heat the chocolate in a microwave-safe glass bowl in 30-second increments, stirring in between each session, for 1½ minutes at most. Then remove the bowl from the microwave and stir. The residual heat will melt any solids. For smooth, shiny chocolate, melt it with a tablespoon or two of solid coconut oil. This helps keep the chocolate from seizing up or curdling and gives it a glossy sheen.

ABOUT THE RECIPES

My hope is that these recipes will appeal to both novice dessert makers and those with years of experience. Each chapter focuses on a particular type of dessert, from Cookies and Bars (page 17) to Cakes and Cupcakes (page 39) to Spoon Desserts (page 77) and more, so that you can easily find what you're looking for. At the end of the book I've included a chapter of Sweet Staples (page 107), where you'll find recipes for basics that will be used throughout the book, including a No-Fail Piecrust (page 108), Dairy-Free Buttercream Frosting (page 111), Dark Chocolate Ganache (page 110), and more.

Every recipe has labels to help identify desserts that are free from certain allergens (Gluten-Free, Nut-Free, and Soy-Free), as well as labels that highlight recipes that are great for little bakers (Kid-Friendly); are good for potlucks and bake sales (Big Batch); or have easy cleanup (One Bowl). **A note on allergens:** When dealing with allergens, be sure to read your labels carefully, and use your best judgment. People with tree nut allergies often wonder if they should avoid coconut. My understanding is that even though the Food and Drug Administration recognizes it as a tree nut, it is a fruit. While allergic reactions have been documented, most people with tree nut allergies can safely eat coconut. I've labeled recipes containing coconut as "Nut-Free," but if you are allergic to tree nuts, talk to your allergist before adding coconut to your diet.

I've also included tips and tricks throughout the recipes:

Ingredient tip: highlights a particular ingredient with informative or interesting info

Variation tip: suggests an optional addition or substitution for the recipe to change the flavor or presentation or to remove an allergen

Make-ahead tip: offers instructions for storage or making components in advance

Lighten-up tip: provides ideas for substitutions to lower the sugar, oil, or fat content of a dessert

Time-saving tip: gives options to save prep time with store-bought ingredients

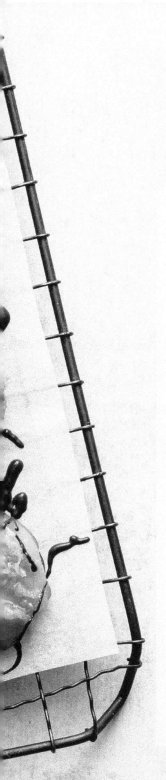

2

COOKIES
AND BARS

Chocolate, Caramel, and Coconut Rings

Soft and Chewy Lemon and Poppy Seed Cookies

PREP TIME: 20 minutes · **COOK TIME:** 15 minutes · **INACTIVE TIME:** 25 minutes

BIG BATCH, NUT-FREE, SOY-FREE · MAKES: 20 cookies

I love the classic combination of lemon and poppy seed. Bright, tangy lemon plays so well with these savory little seeds, and this cookie is the perfect canvas to highlight these delicious flavors. This recipe produces a soft, light cookie that is perfect for serving with brunch or at a summer picnic or potluck. This recipe doubles easily, which makes it a fantastic choice for your next cookie swap or bake sale too!

FOR THE COOKIES

2 tablespoons hot water

1 tablespoon ground flaxseed

2 cups all-purpose flour

2 teaspoons baking powder

1 teaspoon cornstarch

½ teaspoon salt

1 cup granulated sugar

½ cup plus 2 tablespoons vegan butter, at room temperature

Zest of 2 lemons

2 tablespoons fresh lemon juice

2 tablespoons poppy seeds

1 tablespoon agave nectar

1. Preheat the oven to 350°F. Line 2 large rimmed baking sheets with parchment paper.

2. **Make the cookies:** In a small bowl, combine the water and flaxseed. Let stand for about 5 minutes, or until thickened. Meanwhile, in a medium bowl, combine the flour, baking powder, cornstarch, and salt.

3. Using an electric hand mixer in a bowl, beat the sugar, butter, and zest on medium-high for about 3 minutes, or until light and fluffy. Add the flaxseed mixture, lemon juice, poppy seeds, and agave. Mix until just incorporated. Reduce the speed to low and gradually add the flour mixture until just combined.

4. Using a 2-inch cookie scoop, drop even amounts of the dough 2 inches apart onto the prepared baking sheets. (If you don't have a cookie scoop, see the chart on page 10.) Gently flatten with your hands or the bottom of a glass until ¼- to ⅓-inch thick. Bake for 12 minutes, or until lightly golden. Remove from the oven, let cool for 5 minutes, then transfer to a wire rack to cool completely.

FOR THE GLAZE

1 cup powdered sugar

1 tablespoon fresh
  lemon juice

5. **Make the glaze:** Meanwhile, in a small bowl, combine the sugar and lemon juice. Stir for about 5 minutes, or until a thick glaze forms. Using a tablespoon, spoon the glaze in a circular motion on top of each cookie, keeping it away from the edge. Let set for about 20 minutes, or until the glaze has dried.

Lighten-up tip: Replace ½ cup granulated sugar with unsweetened applesauce to limit the amount of refined sugar.

Bakery-Style Sprinkle Cookies

PREP TIME: 25 minutes · **COOK TIME:** 10 minutes · **INACTIVE TIME:** 25 minutes

BIG BATCH, KID-FRIENDLY, NUT-FREE, SOY-FREE · MAKES: 48 cookies

Life is just better with sprinkles. Especially when they coat soft, buttery cookies. You know the kind I'm talking about: the ones always on display at the front of any good bakery. When I was growing up, my great-aunt and great-uncle owned that kind of bakery, and when my grandfather took me to visit, the bakers in the back would sneak me sprinkle cookies. Now I get to create similar memories for my kids—and they get to help bake them too!

3 cups all-purpose flour
1 teaspoon
   baking powder
½ teaspoon salt
¼ teaspoon baking soda
1¼ cups granulated sugar
1 cup vegan butter, at
   room temperature
½ ounce vegan cream
   cheese, at room
   temperature
½ cup unsweetened
   plant-based milk
2 teaspoons
   vanilla extract
1 cup rainbow sprinkles

1. Preheat the oven to 375°F. Line 2 large rimmed baking sheets with parchment paper.

2. In a medium bowl, combine the flour, baking powder, salt, and baking soda.

3. Using an electric hand mixer in a bowl or a stand mixer with paddle attachment, beat the sugar, butter, and cream cheese on medium for 3 to 5 minutes, or until fluffy. Add the milk and vanilla. Mix until combined. Reduce the speed to low and slowly mix in the flour mixture until incorporated. Refrigerate for 15 to 20 minutes.

4. Pour the sprinkles into a shallow bowl. Scoop up about 2 tablespoons of the dough and roll between the palms of your hand to form a ball shape. Toss in the sprinkles to coat. Place the dough on a prepared baking sheet. Repeat with the remaining dough, spacing at least 2 inches apart, until both sheets are full. (There will still be dough left over.)

5. Using the bottom of a glass, gently press down until the dough is about ½-inch thickness. Add any remaining sprinkles to fill in any blank spots. Bake for 9 to 10 minutes, or until very lightly golden on the bottom. You don't want the tops to darken.

6. Remove from the oven, leaving the oven on. Let cool for 5 minutes, then transfer to a wire rack to cool completely. Replace the parchment paper and repeat with the remaining dough.

Lighten-up tip: Replace ½ cup vegan butter with ½ cup unsweetened applesauce to make these cookies lower in fat.

Variation tip: Out of sprinkles? Use dairy-free mini chocolate chips!

New York–Style Black and White Cookies

PREP TIME: 20 minutes · **COOK TIME:** 15 minutes · **INACTIVE TIME:** 40 minutes

BIG BATCH, NUT-FREE, SOY-FREE · MAKES: 36 cookies

To New Yorkers, the black and white cookie is as iconic as the Statue of Liberty or the Empire State Building. It's a piece of history wrapped up in a delicious cake-like cookie. One of the original recipes is from Glaser's Bake Shop in Manhattan and dates back to the early 1900s. The cookie is still available in bakeries and bodegas across New York today. This vegan version should capture the heart of any die-hard New Yorker, vegan or not.

FOR THE COOKIES

3⅓ cups all-purpose flour

1½ teaspoons
   baking powder

1½ teaspoons salt

1¼ cups plant-based
   milk, divided

2 teaspoons
   vanilla extract

1½ teaspoons lemon zest

1⅔ cups granulated sugar

1 cup vegan butter, at
   room temperature

1. Preheat the oven to 375°F. Line 2 large rimmed baking sheets with parchment paper.

2. **Make the cookies:** In a medium bowl, combine the flour, baking powder, and salt. In a small bowl, combine 1 cup of milk, the vanilla, and zest.

3. Using an electric hand mixer in a large bowl or a stand mixer with paddle attachment, beat the sugar and butter on medium-high, scraping down the sides occasionally, for 3 to 4 minutes, or until fluffy. Add the remaining ¼ cup of milk and beat until incorporated. Starting and ending with the flour mixture, gradually add the flour mixture and milk mixture, mixing until just combined after each addition.

4. Using a 2-inch cookie scoop, drop 3-tablespoon scoopfuls of the dough about 2 inches apart onto the prepared baking sheets. (If you don't have a cookie scoop, see the chart on page 10.) Bake for 10 to 12 minutes, or until the edges are lightly golden. Remove from the oven. Transfer to wire racks and let cool completely. Repeat with any remaining dough.

FOR THE VANILLA GLAZE

12 cups powdered sugar

1 cup plant-based milk

1 tablespoon
   vanilla extract

FOR THE CHOCOLATE GLAZE

9 cups powdered sugar

3 cups unsweetened
   cocoa powder

1½ cups plant-based milk

5. **Make the vanilla glaze:** In a bowl, whisk the sugar, milk, and vanilla. Place rimmed baking sheets underneath the wire racks (keeping the cookies on the racks) and spoon the glaze over the cookies, letting the excess drip down. Let stand for 10 to 15 minutes to harden.

6. **Make the chocolate glaze:** In a bowl, whisk the sugar, cocoa powder, and milk. Spoon the glaze over half of each cookie, letting the excess drip down. Let stand for about 5 minutes to set.

Lighten-up tip: Lower the fat content by replacing the butter with unsweetened applesauce.

Chocolate, Caramel, and Coconut Rings

PREP TIME: 1 hour · **COOK TIME:** 25 minutes · **INACTIVE TIME:** 1 hour 15 minutes

BIG BATCH, NUT-FREE, SOY-FREE · MAKES: 48 cookies

This cookie is a take on an iconic Girl Scout cookie that's the second highest–selling cookie during their cookie campaigns. (Thin Mints remain their number-one seller—in case you were wondering.) A sugar cookie ring coated with caramel, coconut, and chocolate is an irresistible treat that is worth repeating in your own kitchen any time of year. To make this cookie, you'll need two different sizes of round cookie cutters. I recommend using 2-inch and 1-inch cutters.

FOR THE COOKIES

2 cups all-purpose flour, plus more for rolling

¼ teaspoon baking powder

½ teaspoon salt

1 cup vegan butter, at room temperature

½ cup granulated sugar

2 tablespoons plant-based milk

½ teaspoon vanilla extract

FOR THE TOPPING

3 cups shredded unsweetened coconut

¾ cup vegan butter, at room temperature

½ cup granulated sugar

14 ounces condensed coconut milk

3 tablespoons light corn syrup

1 cup dairy-free chocolate chips

1. **Make the cookies:** In a medium bowl, combine the flour, baking powder, and salt.

2. Using an electric hand mixer in a large bowl, beat the butter and sugar on medium-high for about 5 minutes, or until light and fluffy.

3. Reduce the speed to low and gradually add the flour mixture, scraping down the bowl after each addition. Add the milk and vanilla. Mix until combined.

4. Turn the dough out onto a flat surface and divide in half. Form both halves into discs, wrap each in plastic wrap, and refrigerate for about 45 minutes, or until firm.

5. Preheat the oven to 350°F. Line 2 large rimmed baking sheets with parchment paper.

6. Lightly flour a flat surface and a rolling pin. Roll the first disc of dough until about ⅛ inch thick. Using a 2-inch round cookie cutter, cut into circles. Place a 1-inch round cookie cutter in the center of each and cut out a smaller circle to make rings. Put the rings on a prepared baking sheet and repeat with the remaining dough.

7. Bake for 10 to 12 minutes, or until very lightly browned. Remove from the oven and let cool completely on a wire rack.

8. **Make the topping:** Line a rimmed baking sheet with parchment paper. Spread the shredded coconut on the prepared baking sheet and toast in the oven, stirring frequently to prevent burning, for 7 to 10 minutes, or until lightly browned. Remove from the oven.

9. Meanwhile, in a medium saucepan, combine the butter and sugar and stir over medium heat until melted. Stir in the condensed milk and syrup. Bring to a boil, then immediately reduce the heat to a simmer. Cook, stirring constantly, for 7 to 10 minutes, or until deep golden. Reserve a ¼ of the caramel sauce in a small bowl and add the toasted coconut to the remaining sauce.

10. Spread the reserved caramel onto each cookie, then top with the coconut-caramel sauce, pressing down to make sure it sticks. Let cool for 30 minutes.

11. In a heat-proof glass bowl set over a pot filled with 2 to 3 inches of simmering water, heat the chocolate chips, stirring frequently, until melted. (Or melt in the microwave in 30-second intervals until smooth, stirring in between.)

12. Dip the bottom of each cookie into the chocolate and place on wax paper to set. Using a fork, drizzle the tops of the cookies with more melted chocolate. Let sit until hardened.

Lighten-up tip: Swap out ½ cup butter in the cookie dough for unsweetened applesauce to reduce the amount of fat but still keep the buttery texture.

Variation tip: The caramel topping makes for a chewy, caramel treat on its own. Once cooked, stir in ½ teaspoon vanilla extract and spread on a large lined rimmed baking sheet. Sprinkle with a pinch sea salt and let cool completely (1 to 2 hours). Cut into small squares and wrap in wax paper.

Cinnamon-Pecan Swirls

PREP TIME: 1 hour 15 minutes · **COOK TIME:** 30 minutes
INACTIVE TIME: 1 hour 20 minutes

BIG BATCH, SOY-FREE · **MAKES:** 48 to 72 cookies

These cookies always remind me of cinnamon rolls but are much easier to make. Cinnamon, sugar, and chopped pecans are swirled around a cookie dough, giving them a beautiful and festive look and light, buttery taste. They're a great choice for holiday cookie swaps or parties, and they freeze really well for those last-minute "cookie emergencies."

1¼ cups all-purpose flour, plus more for rolling

¼ teaspoon salt

1 cup pecans, finely chopped

⅓ cup granulated sugar

1 teaspoon ground cinnamon

½ cup vegan butter, at room temperature

½ cup vegan cream cheese, at room temperature

1. Line 2 large rimmed baking sheets with parchment paper. In a small bowl, combine the flour and salt. In another small bowl, mix the pecans, sugar, and cinnamon.

2. Using an electric hand mixer in a large bowl or a stand mixer with paddle attachment, beat the butter and cream cheese on medium for about 2 minutes, or until creamy. Reduce the speed to low and slowly add the flour mixture, scraping down the bowl as needed. Turn the dough out onto a sheet of plastic wrap and form into a rectangle. Freeze for 30 minutes.

3. Lightly flour a flat surface and a rolling pin, and gently roll the dough out into a roughly 15-by-12-inch rectangle. Sprinkle the pecan mixture evenly across.

4. Starting from one long side, tightly roll the dough into a log. Brush the last ½ inch of the dough with some water to help the edge stick. Cut in half and transfer both logs to 1 baking sheet. Cover with plastic wrap and freeze for 45 minutes.

5. Preheat the oven to 400°F. Remove 1 log from the freezer and using a serrated knife, cut into ¼-inch-thick rounds. Lay the rounds about ½ inch apart on the remaining prepared baking sheet. Bake for 12 to 14 minutes, or until lightly browned. Remove from the oven, let cool for 5 minutes, then transfer to a wire rack to continue cooling. Repeat with the remaining log.

Make-ahead tip: Wrap unbaked dough in plastic wrap before placing in a freezer-safe resealable bag, and freeze for up to 3 months. Defrost in the refrigerator overnight or on the counter for an hour before slicing and baking. Keep baked cookies in a freezer-safe resealable bag and defrost at room temperature until soft enough to eat.

Italian Rainbow Cookies

PREP TIME: 45 minutes · **COOK TIME:** 25 minutes · **INACTIVE TIME:** 4 hours 45 minutes

BIG BATCH, KID-FRIENDLY, SOY-FREE · MAKES: 18 to 24 cookies

Rainbow cookies, or *tricolore* cookies, are an homage to the Italian flag and were brought over to America in the early 1900s by Italian immigrants. Colorful layers of almond cake are layered with fruit jam (raspberry is the classic version), then covered in chocolate. These cookies are as fun to look at as they are to eat. Traditional rainbow cookies call for almond paste, which can be bought in stores, but more often than not, it contains eggs. I've adapted this recipe to use a classic vegan almond cake instead.

FOR THE COOKIES

2 cups all-purpose flour
1 cup almond flour
1 cup granulated sugar
2 teaspoons
   baking powder
1 teaspoon salt
1½ cups almond milk
½ cup vegetable oil
½ teaspoon
   almond extract
2 to 4 drops vegan green
   gel food coloring
4 to 6 drops vegan red
   gel food coloring
1 (15-ounce) jar apricot or
   raspberry jam, divided

FOR THE CHOCOLATE TOPPING

1½ cups dairy-free
   chocolate chips
1 tablespoon solid
   coconut oil

1. Preheat the oven to 350°F. Line 3 (9-by-13-by-1½-inch) rimmed baking sheets with parchment paper, leaving 2 to 3 inches hanging over all sides.

2. **Make the cookies:** In a large bowl, combine the all-purpose flour, almond flour, sugar, baking powder, and salt. Add the milk, oil, and almond extract. Whisk until smooth.

3. Using a kitchen scale, divide the batter evenly into 3 bowls. Add 2 drops of green food coloring to one bowl and whisk to combine, adding more if needed to achieve a deep green color. Add 4 drops of red food coloring to the second bowl, whisking to combine, and adding more if needed to achieve a deep red (not pink) color. Leave the third bowl as is.

4. Pour the bowl of green batter onto one prepared baking sheet, using an offset spatula to spread evenly. Repeat with the remaining 2 bowls of batter and remaining 2 baking sheets. Bake for 15 to 18 minutes, or until a toothpick inserted in the center comes out clean. Remove from the oven, and let cool completely, about 30 minutes.

Continued >

5. Spread half of the jam evenly across the green layer. Gently lift the plain layer out of its sheet by holding on to the edges of parchment and lifting it up. Turn it upside-down and place it on the green layer, gently peeling away the paper. Top evenly with the remaining jam, and repeat to place the red layer on top of the plain layer.

6. Place a piece of parchment paper bigger than the cake on a large rimmed baking sheet. Put the lined baking sheet on top of the cake, and turn it over so that the sheet holding the green layer is facing up. Remove that sheet, tightly cover the cake in plastic wrap, and place that sheet back on top. Refrigerate, evenly weighing it down by placing cans or heavy items on top. Chill for at least 4 hours. Unwrap and slice ¼ to ½ inch off the ends to create clean edges.

7. Line a rimmed baking sheet with parchment paper, and place a wire rack on top. Transfer the cake to the wire rack.

8. **Make the chocolate topping:** In a heat-proof glass bowl set over a pot filled with 2 to 3 inches of simmering water, heat the chocolate chips and oil, stirring frequently, until melted. (Or melt in the microwave in 30-second intervals until smooth, stirring in between.)

9. Pour over the entire cake, smoothing the top and sides as best you can using an offset spatula. Let set for 15 minutes, or until the chocolate has hardened.

10. Slice the cake in half horizontally, then cut each half into rectangular cookies about 1 inch wide.

> **Lighten-up tip:** Reduce the amount of sugar in the cookies by replacing 1 cup granulated sugar with 1 cup unsweetened applesauce and reducing the amount of almond milk to 1¼ cups.

Apple Pie Cookies

PREP TIME: 20 minutes · **COOK TIME:** 15 minutes

KID-FRIENDLY, NUT-FREE, SOY-FREE · MAKES: 24 cookies

These autumnal cookies have a slightly crispy exterior and a soft, apple-studded interior that make me think of apple pie—but with less work and less cleanup. For this recipe, choose a crisp, sturdy apple that won't turn mushy when baked, like Honeycrisp or Granny Smith.

FOR THE COOKIES

2 tablespoons hot water

1 tablespoon ground
  flaxseed

1¼ cups all-purpose flour

2 teaspoons
  baking powder

¼ teaspoon salt

½ cup vegan butter, at
  room temperature

½ cup granulated sugar

½ cup brown sugar

1 teaspoon vanilla extract

½ medium apple, peeled
  and finely diced

FOR THE COATING

3 tablespoons
  granulated sugar

1 teaspoon ground
  cinnamon

¼ teaspoon
  ground nutmeg

¼ teaspoon
  ground ginger

1. Preheat the oven to 350°F. Line 2 large rimmed baking sheets with parchment paper.

2. **Make the cookies:** In a small bowl, combine the water and flaxseed. Let sit for about 5 minutes. In another large bowl, whisk the flour, baking powder, and salt.

3. Using an electric hand mixer in a large bowl or a stand mixer with paddle attachment, cream the butter, granulated sugar, and brown sugar on medium-high for about 3 minutes, or until combined. Add the flaxseed mixture, vanilla, and apple. Stir to combine. Turn the mixer to low and slowly add the flour mixture, scraping down the bowl as needed.

4. **Make the coating:** In a small bowl, combine the sugar, cinnamon, nutmeg, and ginger.

5. Using a 1-inch cookie scoop or a tablespoon, scoop the dough and roll it into balls. Roll each ball in the cinnamon-sugar mixture to coat. Place the balls about 2 inches apart on the prepared baking sheets, flatten slightly, and bake for 12 minutes, or until the tops and bottoms are lightly golden. Remove from the oven. Let cool completely.

Lighten-up tip: Substitute ½ cup granulated sugar for ½ cup unsweetened applesauce. You'll not only cut down on sugar, but you'll also add more apple flavor.

Blueberry Cheesecake Bars

PREP TIME: 30 minutes · **COOK TIME:** 20 minutes · **INACTIVE TIME:** 4 hours

SOY-FREE, NUT-FREE · MAKES: 12 bars

I like to call these a "low-bake" dessert. Though the base requires a few minutes of oven time, the filling needs no baking at all. Many vegan cheesecake desserts use cashews as the base, but for a nut-free version, I use vegan cream cheese, which gives these bars a creamier and more authentic feel.

FOR THE CRUST

9 vegan Graham crackers
⅛ teaspoon salt
¼ cup vegan
   butter, melted

FOR THE FILLING

15 ounces vegan cream
   cheese, at room
   temperature
⅔ cup granulated sugar
½ cup coconut
   oil, melted
⅓ cup fresh lime juice

FOR THE TOPPING

2 cups fresh or thawed
   frozen blueberries
½ cup plus 2 tablespoons
   water, divided
½ cup granulated sugar
2 tablespoons fresh
   lemon juice
1 tablespoon lemon zest
2 tablespoons cornstarch

1. Preheat the oven to 350°F. Line an 8-by-8-inch baking pan with parchment paper, leaving about ½ inch hanging over all sides.

2. **Make the crust:** In a food processor, combine the crackers and salt. Process into fine crumbs. Slowly stream in the butter while processing. Transfer to the pan and press down firmly to form an even crust. Bake for 5 to 7 minutes, or until golden brown. Remove from the oven. Let cool.

3. **Make the filling:** Using an electric hand mixer in a large bowl or a stand mixer with paddle attachment, beat the cream cheese, sugar, and oil on medium-high for about 5 minutes, or until well mixed. Add the lime juice and beat until creamy. Pour on top of the crust and refrigerate.

4. **Make the topping:** In a medium saucepan, bring the blueberries, ½ cup of water, the sugar, lemon juice, and zest to a low boil.

5. In a small bowl, combine the cornstarch and the remaining 2 tablespoons of water. Slowly pour into the saucepan, stirring as you pour, and simmer for about 5 minutes, or until thick enough to coat the back of a spoon. Let cool.

6. Top the cheesecake with the sauce, then refrigerate for at least 4 hours to set. Cut into bars just before serving.

Lemon Squares

PREP TIME: 15 minutes · **COOK TIME:** 30 minutes · **INACTIVE TIME:** 2 hours 20 minutes

BIG BATCH, NUT-FREE, SOY-FREE · MAKES: 16 squares

Rich, buttery shortbread, tart and creamy lemon curd filling, and a dusting of powdered sugar make this a fantastic spring or summer treat. It took a little while, but I've finally perfected a vegan version of a luscious lemon filling that tastes so close to a traditional lemon curd, it's hard to tell the difference!

1 cup all-purpose flour

½ cup vegan butter, at room temperature

1¾ cups granulated sugar, divided

1¼ cups full-fat coconut milk

¾ cup fresh lemon juice (about 4 to 5 lemons)

5 tablespoons cornstarch

2 teaspoons lemon zest

3 tablespoons powdered sugar, for dusting

1 lemon, sliced into half moons, for garnish

1. Preheat the oven to 350°F. Line an 8-by-8-inch baking pan with parchment paper, leaving about ½ inch hanging over all sides.

2. In a large bowl, combine the flour, butter, and ¼ cup of granulated sugar. Using a pastry cutter, cut the butter into the flour until it resembles small crumbs and the dough sticks together when pressed between your fingers. Press evenly into the prepared pan and bake for 12 to 14 minutes, or until just firm but not brown.

3. Meanwhile, in a medium saucepan over medium heat, combine the remaining 1½ cups of granulated sugar, the milk, lemon juice, cornstarch, and zest. Whisk well to ensure the cornstarch is fully dissolved. Cook, whisking and watching constantly, for about 7 minutes, or until the sugar has fully dissolved and the mixture has thickened into a curd-like consistency.

4. Spread the filling evenly over the crust and bake for 15 minutes, or until the top is just bubbling around the edges. Remove from the oven, let cool for 15 to 20 minutes, then refrigerate for at least 2 hours. When set, remove from the pan and dust with the powdered sugar. Cut into squares and garnish with the lemon slices.

Make-ahead tip: These bars get better (and firmer) the longer they set, so make them a day in advance. Keep the pan covered in the refrigerator overnight, and cut and garnish just before serving.

Chocolate and Coconut Dream Bars

PREP TIME: 10 minutes · **COOK TIME:** 30 minutes · **INACTIVE TIME:** 1 hour 15 minutes

BIG BATCH, KID-FRIENDLY, ONE BOWL · **MAKES:** 12 to 16 bars

Dream bars, seven-layer bars, million dollar bars—these treats have many names, but they should really be called First Dessert to Disappear from the Buffet Bars since they're always a hit! Chocolate, peanuts, pretzels, and a gooey, rich layer of coconut held together on a cookie-crumb crust—they hit all the notes of sweet and salty, smooth and crunchy. It's also a great recipe for little helpers to make; just watch out for tiny hands sneaking chocolate chips when you're not looking!

1½ cups vegan chocolate sandwich cookie crumbs

3 tablespoons vegan butter, melted

¾ cup dairy-free mini chocolate chips

¾ cup shredded unsweetened coconut

½ cup crushed pretzels

¼ cup chopped peanuts

1¼ cups canned coconut milk

1. Preheat the oven to 350°F. Line an 8-by-8-inch baking pan with parchment paper, making sure it's long enough to hang over all sides.

2. In a medium bowl, mix the cookie crumbs with the butter until combined. Press the crumb mixture into the bottom of the prepared baking pan to completely cover.

3. Sprinkle the chocolate chips, coconut, pretzels, and peanuts on top, then pour the coconut milk over the entire dish.

4. Bake for 30 minutes. Remove from the oven, let cool for 10 to 15 minutes, then refrigerate for 30 minutes to 1 hour to firm up. Slice into bars and serve.

Variation tip: Swap out ¼ of the dairy-free chocolate chips for dairy-free white chocolate chips. Many kosher brands of white chocolate, such as King David, are vegan. You can also swap out the chocolate sandwich cookie crumbs for vegan Graham crackers to create a blondie-style crust.

Rocky Road Squares

PREP TIME: 10 minutes · **COOK TIME:** 25 minutes

BIG BATCH, ONE BOWL · MAKES: 32 squares

These chewy, chocolatey squares are super easy to make and are always a game-day or picnic crowd-pleaser! Mini vegan marshmallows make all the difference in this dessert and are worth looking for in specialty grocers or online.

½ cup vegan butter, melted

1½ cups vegan Graham cracker crumbs (about 10 Graham crackers)

1½ cups shredded unsweetened coconut

1½ cups chopped almonds

2½ cups dairy-free chocolate chips, divided

1½ cups mini vegan marshmallows, such as Dandies brand

1 (14-ounce) can condensed coconut milk

1. Preheat the oven to 350°F.

2. In a 9-by-13-inch baking pan, mix the butter and cracker crumbs to combine. Press firmly into the bottom to form a crust.

3. Layer the coconut, almonds, 2 cups of chocolate chips, and the marshmallows on top. Drizzle with the condensed milk.

4. Bake for 25 minutes, or until golden brown. Remove from the oven and top with the remaining ½ cup of chocolate chips. Let cool completely before cutting into squares.

Variation tip: Classic rocky road usually includes almonds, but this dessert can easily be adapted for nut-free diets by swapping them out for crushed pretzels, which pair really well with chocolate and offer the same crunch.

Chocolate Éclair Bars

PREP TIME: 20 minutes · **INACTIVE TIME:** 8 hours

SOY-FREE · MAKES: 15 bars

This is a real showstopper dessert. Graham cracker layers surround a luscious, filling that's a cross between pastry cream and custard, topped with a layer of velvety chocolate. It takes a bit of prep, but the bulk of the time is just refrigeration.

FOR THE ÉCLAIRS

15 to 20 vegan Graham crackers, divided

3½ cups almond milk or other plant-based milk

2 (3.4-ounce) packages instant vegan vanilla pudding mix

3 cups Coconut Whipped Cream (page 115) or store-bought

FOR THE TOPPING

¼ cup dairy-free chocolate chips

2 tablespoons vegan butter, at room temperature

1½ cups powdered sugar

3 tablespoons almond milk or other plant-based milk

1 teaspoon light corn syrup

1 teaspoon vanilla extract

1. **Make the éclairs:** In a 9-by-13-inch baking pan, layer half of the crackers, breaking in half if needed to fit.

2. In a large bowl, combine the milk and instant pudding mix. Whisk for 2 minutes. Let stand for 2 to 3 minutes. Gently fold in the whipped cream, being careful not to deflate, and spread evenly over the layer of crackers. Top with the remaining crackers and refrigerate.

3. **Make the topping:** In a heat-proof glass bowl set over a pot filled with 2 to 3 inches of simmering water, heat the chocolate chips and butter, stirring frequently, until melted. (Or melt in the microwave in 30-second intervals until combined and smooth, stirring in between.) Stir in the sugar, milk, corn syrup, and vanilla.

4. Spread over the layer of crackers, cover, and refrigerate for at least 8 hours. When ready to serve, cut into squares.

Lighten-up tip: Choose an unsweetened plant-based milk to prevent adding sugar to an already sweet dessert.

Time-saving tip: You can use store-bought whipped cream or frozen coconut topping for this recipe.

CAKES AND CUPCAKES

Black Forest Cake

Snickerdoodle Cupcakes with Brown Sugar Buttercream

PREP TIME: 15 minutes · COOK TIME: 20 minutes · INACTIVE TIME: 20 minutes

BIG BATCH, KID-FRIENDLY, NUT-FREE, SOY-FREE · MAKES: 24 cupcakes

These light and fluffy cupcakes trace their origin to the classic snickerdoodle—a soft, pillowy sugar cookie coated in a mix of cinnamon and sugar. I use unsweetened applesauce as a replacement for eggs in this recipe and greatly reduced the amount of sugar because the applesauce adds a natural sweetness and also helps keep the cupcakes fluffy and moist. Top these beauties with a cloud of brown sugar buttercream.

FOR THE CUPCAKES

3 cups all-purpose flour

1 tablespoon baking powder

1 tablespoon ground cinnamon

½ teaspoon salt

1¼ cups granulated sugar

1 cup vegan butter, at room temperature

2 teaspoons vanilla extract

1 cup unsweetened applesauce

1 cup plant-based milk, divided

1. Preheat the oven to 350°F. Line 2 standard muffin tins with paper liners.

2. **Make the cupcakes:** In a large bowl, combine the flour, baking powder, cinnamon, and salt.

3. Using an electric hand mixer in another large bowl, beat the sugar and butter on medium-high for about 5 minutes, or until light and fluffy. Add the vanilla, then applesauce, ¼ cup at a time, scraping down the bowl as needed.

4. Reduce the speed to low and add ⅓ of the flour mixture, mixing until incorporated, followed by ½ cup of milk. Add another ⅓ of the flour mixture, followed by the remaining ½ cup of milk and the remaining flour mixture. Beat until fully combined.

5. Fill each muffin cup ¾ full. Bake for 18 to 20 minutes, rotating halfway through, or until a toothpick inserted in the center comes out clean. Remove from the oven, and let cool completely, about 20 minutes.

FOR THE FROSTING

1½ cups vegan butter, at room temperature

2 tablespoons packed brown sugar

1 teaspoon ground cinnamon

½ teaspoon vanilla extract

4 cups powdered sugar, divided

6. **Make the frosting:** Using an electric hand mixer in a large bowl, beat the butter, brown sugar, cinnamon, and vanilla on medium for about 5 minutes, or until light and fluffy. Reduce the speed to low, and slowly incorporate 1 cup of powdered sugar, beating for 1 minute. Increase the speed to medium and beat for 3 to 4 minutes. Repeat in 1-cup increments with the remaining 3 cups of powdered sugar.

7. Using an offset spatula or a piping bag fitted with a large star or round tip, frost the cupcakes.

Lighten-up tip: Swap out the butter in the cupcake batter for 1 packed cup mashed banana.

Dreamy Cream-Filled Chocolate Cupcakes

PREP TIME: 20 minutes · **COOK TIME:** 20 minutes · **INACTIVE TIME:** 45 minutes

BIG BATCH, KID-FRIENDLY, NUT-FREE · MAKES: 24 cupcakes

These cupcakes practically scream childhood to me. Opening my lunch bag and finding one of these was the grade-school equivalent of winning the lottery. We're talking instant sugar rush (and inevitable sugar crash shortly after). I've modified this recipe to make it a little less sweet and given it a grown-up boost by using a bit of brewed coffee in the batter, which really helps bring out the chocolate flavor. But don't worry—it's still totally kid-friendly.

1½ cups all-purpose flour

1 cup granulated sugar

¾ cup Dutch-process cocoa powder

1½ teaspoons baking soda

¾ teaspoon baking powder

1 cup soy buttermilk

½ cup brewed coffee, hot

½ cup unsweetened applesauce

1 teaspoon vanilla extract

2 cups Coconut Whipped Cream (page 115) or store-bought, chilled until needed

1 cup dairy-free semisweet chocolate chips

⅔ cup coconut or soy cream

1 cup powdered sugar, plus more as needed

1 tablespoon soy milk

1. Preheat the oven to 350°F. Line 2 standard muffin tins with paper liners.

2. In a large bowl, combine the flour, granulated sugar, cocoa powder, baking soda, and baking powder. Add the buttermilk, coffee, applesauce, and vanilla. Whisk to combine.

3. Scoop into the prepared muffin tins, filling each cup about ½ full. Bake for 18 to 20 minutes, or until a toothpick inserted in the center comes out clean. Remove from the oven. Let cool completely.

4. Transfer the whipped cream to a piping bag fitted with a medium round tip, or a resealable bag with the corner snipped off. Using the end of a spatula or whisk, push a hole into the middle of each cupcake. Fill with the cream. Freeze the cupcakes for about 15 minutes.

5. In a heat-proof glass bowl set over a pot filled with 2 to 3 inches of simmering water, heat the chocolate chips and coconut cream, stirring frequently, until melted. (Or melt in the microwave in 30-second intervals until smooth, stirring in between.)

6. In a small bowl, whisk the powdered sugar and soy milk until smooth and icing falls off the whisk in ribbons. If too thin, add more sugar, 1 tablespoon at a time, until the desired consistency is reached. Transfer to a piping bag fitted with a small round tip, or a resealable bag with the corner snipped off to make a very small opening.

7. Dip or spoon the melted chocolate ganache on top of each cupcake. Let set for 10 minutes, then pipe icing loops across the center of each cupcake and let set for 15 minutes.

Ingredient tip: To make vegan buttermilk, add 1 tablespoon fresh lemon juice or white vinegar to 1 cup plant-based milk and let sit at room temperature for about 5 minutes, or until the top of the milk starts to curdle. Stir, then use as directed in your recipe.

Lighten-up tip: Use this avocado-chocolate frosting recipe for less sugar than the ganache: In a blender or food processor, combine 2 really ripe avocados, ½ cup Dutch-process cocoa powder, ¼ cup maple syrup, ¼ teaspoon vanilla extract, and ⅛ teaspoon salt. Blend until smooth.

Ice Cream Sundae Cupcake Cones

PREP TIME: 20 minutes · **COOK TIME:** 25 minutes

BIG BATCH, KID-FRIENDLY, NUT-FREE · MAKES: 24 cupcake cones

I'm a huge fan of dessert imposters, aka a dessert that looks like one thing but is really another. These ice cream cone cupcakes are the ultimate dessert imposter. At a quick glance, they look just like delicious soft-serve cones, but one bite reveals a delicious vanilla-confetti cupcake topped with marshmallow fluff frosting, all nestled in a crunchy ice cream cone. The trick to making vegan marshmallow fluff is a secret ingredient called aquafaba, or the brine from a can of chickpeas. See page 4 for more information.

24 flat-bottomed ice cream cones

2½ cups all-purpose flour

2¼ cups granulated sugar, divided

1 cup vegan confetti sprinkles or chips

1 tablespoon plus 1 teaspoon baking powder

1 teaspoon salt

¼ cup vegan butter, at room temperature

1 cup unsweetened soy milk

⅔ cup grapeseed or light vegetable oil

½ cup unsweetened applesauce

4 teaspoons vanilla extract, divided

3 ounces aquafaba

½ teaspoon cream of tartar

3 tablespoons powdered sugar

1. Preheat the oven to 350°F. Line 2 standard muffin tins with aluminum foil. Place the ice cream cones in the prepared muffin tin cavities, crumpling the aluminum foil if necessary to help stabilize them.

2. In a large bowl, combine the flour, 1½ cups of granulated sugar, the sprinkles, baking powder, and salt. Whisk to combine.

3. Add the butter and, using a pastry cutter, cut the butter into the flour mixture until it resembles coarse cornmeal. (If you don't have a pastry cutter, use 2 knives, cutting in criss-cross motions.)

4. Add the milk, oil, applesauce, and 2 teaspoons of vanilla. Using an electric hand mixer, beat on medium until smooth. Divide the batter evenly among the ice cream cones, filling each one about ¾ full. Don't overfill or they may tip over or become too top-heavy to stand up.

5. Bake for 20 to 23 minutes, or until a toothpick inserted in the center comes out clean. Remove from the oven. Let cool completely.

FOR DECORATING

Vegan chocolate or
   rainbow sprinkles
Vegan maraschino
   cherries

6. Meanwhile, using an electric hand mixer in another large bowl or a stand mixer with whisk attachment, whisk the aquafaba, remaining 2 teaspoons of vanilla, and the cream of tartar on medium-high for 8 to 10 minutes, or until the mixture forms stiff peaks. (If you can turn the bowl upside down and the mix doesn't fall out, you've hit stiff peaks.) Slowly add the powdered sugar and the remaining ¾ cup of granulated sugar and continue beating until dissolved and the fluff has a glossy shine.

7. Transfer to a piping bag fitted with a large round tip, or a resealable bag with the corner snipped off, and pipe onto the cooled cupcakes in a swirling motion to resemble soft-serve. Decorate with sprinkles and cherries on top.

Time-saving tip: Use a box of vegan rainbow chip or funfetti cake mix (see page 8). Follow the directions on the box, substituting 1 ripe mashed banana or ¼ cup unsweetened applesauce per egg, and follow the recipe from step 4. You can replace the marshmallow fluff topping with Dairy-Free Buttercream Frosting (page 111) or store-bought. Many big-brand frostings, such as Betty Crocker, are vegan!

Lighten-up tip: Reduce the amount of sugar by using 1¾ cups granulated sugar and unsweetened vanilla soy milk.

Cookies and Cream Cupcakes

PREP TIME: 20 minutes · **COOK TIME:** 20 minutes · **INACTIVE TIME:** 30 minutes

BIG BATCH, KID-FRIENDLY, NUT-FREE · MAKES: 24 cupcakes

What's better than a cupcake? A cupcake topped with a cookie, of course! These cupcakes are great for kids' parties or bake sales. I've swapped out butter for vegetable oil. It gives the cupcakes a sturdier structure that can support the crushed cookies and remain incredibly moist—even the day after they're made.

FOR THE CUPCAKES

2½ cups all-purpose flour

2½ teaspoons
baking powder

½ teaspoon salt

1 cup granulated sugar

½ cup vegetable oil

½ cup unsweetened
applesauce

1 teaspoon vanilla extract

1¼ cups unsweetened
soy milk, divided

2 cups coarsely crushed
vegan chocolate
sandwich cookies

FOR THE FROSTING

3 cups powdered sugar

1½ cups vegan
chocolate sandwich
cookie crumbs

1 cup vegan butter, at
room temperature

2 tablespoons
unsweetened soy milk

1 teaspoon vanilla extract

24 vegan mini chocolate
sandwich cookies,
for garnish

1. Preheat the oven to 350°F. Line 2 standard muffin tins with paper liners.

2. **Make the cupcakes:** In a large bowl, combine the flour, baking powder, and salt.

3. Using an electric hand mixer in another large bowl, beat the sugar, oil, applesauce, and vanilla on medium for about 3 minutes, or until incorporated and the batter is light and fluffy.

4. Starting and ending with the flour mixture, add about ⅓ of the flour mixture, followed by half of the milk, scraping down the bowl as needed in between additions. Repeat until all ingredients are incorporated. Fold in the crushed cookies.

5. Evenly distribute the batter into the muffin tins, filling each cup about ¾ full. Bake for 18 to 20 minutes, or until a toothpick inserted in the center comes out clean. Remove from the oven. Let cool completely.

6. **Make the frosting:** Using an electric hand mixer in a large bowl, beat the sugar, cookie crumbs, butter, milk, and vanilla on medium until smooth. Pipe or spread over the cupcakes and garnish with the mini cookies.

Lighten-up tip: Halve the amount of granulated sugar in the batter and double the amount of applesauce. Reduce the amount of soy milk by ¼ to ½ cup to adjust for the extra liquid.

Strawberry-Vanilla Baked D'oh-nuts

PREP TIME: 25 minutes · **COOK TIME:** 15 minutes · **INACTIVE TIME:** 40 minutes

KID-FRIENDLY, NUT-FREE · MAKES: 10 donuts

Homemade donuts quicker than the drive to your favorite donut shop—what could be better? No messy deep-frying! These baked donuts are made for experimenting with fillings, flavors, and decorations. See the Variation tip for a few of my go-to swaps.

3 tablespoons vegan butter, melted, plus more for greasing

1¼ cups all-purpose flour

1 cup unsweetened soy milk, divided

½ cup granulated sugar

1½ teaspoons vanilla extract, divided

1 teaspoon baking powder

¼ teaspoon salt

1 cup strawberry jam

1 cup powdered sugar

3 to 4 drops vegan pink gel food coloring

⅓ cup vegan rainbow sprinkles, for decorating

1. Preheat the oven to 350°F. Grease 2 nonstick donut pans. Line a rimmed baking sheet with parchment paper and place a wire rack on top.

2. In a large bowl, combine the flour, ¾ cup of milk, the granulated sugar, butter, 1 teaspoon of vanilla, the baking powder, and salt. Stir until well combined. Spoon into the prepared pans, filling ¼ full. Add a layer of jam to each donut (if your jam is super thick, microwave for 20 to 30 seconds to loosen), then top with more batter, filling ¾ full.

3. Bake for 10 to 12 minutes, or until the tops look set. Remove from the oven, let cool for 5 minutes, then transfer to the wire rack to cool completely.

4. In a medium bowl, combine the powdered sugar, remaining ½ teaspoon of vanilla, ¼ cup of milk, and the food coloring. Whisk until the glaze forms smooth ribbons when drizzled and the color is deep pink.

5. Dip each donut in the glaze and return to the wire rack. Top with the sprinkles and let stand for 10 minutes to set.

Lighten-up tip: Use a reduced-sugar or no-sugar-added jam of your choice or omit it altogether.

Variation tip: For chocolate donuts: Replace ¼ cup flour with ¼ cup cocoa powder. For chocolate glaze: Replace ¼ cup powdered sugar with cocoa powder. For pumpkin spice donuts: Reduce the amount of vanilla to 1 teaspoon and add 1 tablespoon pumpkin spice.

Glazed Blueberry Streusel Coffee Cake

PREP TIME: 15 minutes · **COOK TIME:** 35 minutes · **INACTIVE TIME:** 35 minutes

SOY-FREE · SERVES: 9 to 12

Coffee cake is a classic brunch or afternoon tea dessert. This version is a favorite of mine: a moist, rich cake with the crunch of pecan streusel and a sweet burst of flavor from warm blueberries. I like to use fresh blueberries when in season, but in a pinch, frozen ones work just as well. No need to thaw them first.

FOR THE CAKE

¼ cup plus 2 tablespoons vegan butter, at room temperature, plus more for greasing

1 cup all-purpose flour, plus more for dusting

2 tablespoons hot water

1 tablespoon ground flaxseed

1¼ teaspoons baking powder

¼ teaspoon salt

½ cup granulated sugar

1 cup unsweetened almond milk

1 teaspoon vanilla extract

1¼ cups fresh or frozen blueberries, divided

FOR THE STREUSEL TOPPING

½ cup all-purpose flour

½ cup packed brown sugar

½ cup finely chopped pecans

¼ cup vegan butter, melted

1 teaspoon ground cinnamon

1. Preheat the oven to 350°F. Grease and flour an 8-by-8-inch baking pan.

2. **Make the cake:** In a small bowl, combine the water and flaxseed. Let sit for about 5 minutes.

3. In a medium bowl, combine the flour, baking powder, and salt.

4. Using an electric hand mixer in a large bowl, beat the sugar and butter on medium-high for about 4 minutes, or until light and fluffy. Add the milk, flaxseed mixture, and vanilla and combine well. Slowly add the dry ingredients and mix until smooth.

5. **Make the streusel topping:** In a medium bowl, combine the flour, sugar, pecans, butter, and cinnamon. Stir until well combined.

6. Pour half of the batter into the prepared pan and smooth out to form an even layer. Top with half of the streusel and 1 cup of blueberries, then pour the remaining batter on top. Sprinkle the remaining streusel and ¼ cup of blueberries on top.

7. Bake for 35 minutes, or until a toothpick inserted in the center comes out clean. Remove from the oven, let cool for 20 to 30 minutes, then transfer to a wire rack to cool completely.

FOR THE GLAZE
1 cup powdered sugar
2 tablespoons
  unsweetened
  almond milk

8. **Make the glaze:** In a small bowl, whisk the sugar and milk until thick but pourable. Drizzle over the cooled cake.

Lighten-up tip: Use a packed ½ cup mashed banana or ½ cup unsweetened apple-sauce instead of granulated sugar for the cake.

Variation tip: You can easily make this cake nut-free by swapping out almond milk for any other plant-based milk, such as soy, and by omitting the chopped pecans in the streusel.

Banana Pudding Cake

PREP TIME: 15 minutes · **COOK TIME:** 30 minutes · **INACTIVE TIME:** 30 minutes

NUT-FREE, SOY-FREE · SERVES: 12

This is a fun cake to serve instead of a traditional frosted yellow cake. The addition of banana pudding and mashed banana gives this dessert great flavor. It's a fun one to serve for summer birthdays or get-togethers. Since most boxed yellow cake mixes are not vegan, I've created a scratch version for this recipe.

¼ cup vegan butter, at room temperature, plus more for greasing

2½ cups all-purpose flour

1½ cups granulated sugar

1 tablespoon plus 1 teaspoon baking powder

1 teaspoon salt

2 (3.4-ounce) packages vegan instant banana pudding mix, divided

1½ cups unsweetened coconut milk

1 cup ripe banana, mashed, plus 2 bananas, cut into ½-inch-thick rounds

2 cups coconut cream

2 tablespoons powdered sugar

1. Preheat the oven to 350°F. Grease 2 (9-inch) round cake pans, then line the bottoms with parchment paper and grease again.

2. In a large bowl, combine the flour, granulated sugar, baking powder, and salt. Add the butter and, using a pastry cutter, cut the butter into the flour mixture until it resembles coarse cornmeal. (If you don't have a pastry cutter, use 2 knives, cutting in criss-cross motions.) Add 1 package of instant pudding mix, the milk, and mashed banana. Using an electric hand mixer, mix on medium until smooth.

3. Divide evenly between the prepared pans, smoothing out to form an even layer, and bake for 25 to 30 minutes, or until a toothpick inserted in the center comes out clean. Remove from the oven. Let cool completely.

4. Using an electric hand mixer in a bowl, whip the coconut cream on high. Add the powdered sugar and continue whipping. As the mixture starts to thicken, add the remaining package of pudding mix and mix until smooth and creamy. Refrigerate for at least 30 minutes.

5. Put 1 cake on a cake plate and top with half of the cream filling, smoothing out to form an even layer. Place the remaining cake on top and top with the remaining filling, using an offset spatula to create swirls. Top with the sliced bananas.

Lighten-up tip: Replace ½ cup granulated sugar with ½ cup mashed banana for more banana flavor and lower sugar content.

Make-ahead tip: Combine the first 4 dry ingredients with the vegan butter and store in an airtight container in the refrigerator for up to 2 weeks (or in the freezer for up to 4 months), and you'll always have yellow cake mix on hand.

Carrot Cake with Cream Cheese Frosting

PREP TIME: 30 minutes · **COOK TIME:** 35 minutes · **INACTIVE TIME:** 40 minutes

NUT-FREE, SOY-FREE · **SERVES:** 15

My brother has always loved carrot cake the best of all. He'll always choose it—even over classic chocolate or yellow birthday cakes, whenever he has the chance. It must run in the family, because so does my eldest daughter. I created this cake for one of their birthdays a few years ago, and they've both requested it ever since. Between the two of them, they can polish off an entire cake!

For special occasions, I make a round, layered version with two 9-inch cake pans. To do so, grease and line the pans with parchment paper, divide the batter evenly between the pans and bake for 35 to 40 minutes. Let the cakes cool completely before leveling them (see Technique tip). Place a layer of frosting between the two cakes, and then frost the top and sides.

FOR THE CAKE

1 cup canola oil, plus more for greasing

2 cups all-purpose flour, plus more for dusting

2½ teaspoons ground cinnamon

¾ teaspoon baking soda

½ teaspoon baking powder

½ teaspoon ground ginger

¼ teaspoon salt

¼ teaspoon ground nutmeg

1½ cups granulated sugar

1 cup unsweetened applesauce

3 cups grated carrots

1. Preheat the oven to 350°F. Grease and flour a 9-by-13-inch baking pan.

2. **Make the cake:** In a large bowl, combine the flour, cinnamon, baking soda, baking powder, ginger, salt, and nutmeg. Add the sugar, applesauce, and oil. Using an electric hand mixer, beat on medium until smooth. Gently fold in the carrots.

3. Pour the batter into the prepared pan and bake for 35 minutes, or until a toothpick inserted in the center comes out clean. Remove from the oven. Let cool completely.

FOR THE FROSTING

½ cup vegan butter, at room temperature

1 (8-ounce) container plain vegan cream cheese, slightly softened

1 teaspoon vanilla extract

3 to 5 cups powdered sugar

1 to 2 tablespoons plant-based milk, if needed

4. **Make the frosting:** Using an electric hand mixer in a large bowl, beat the butter, cream cheese, and vanilla on medium-high until fluffy. Add the sugar in 1-cup increments until the frosting is thick and spreadable. (Note that cream cheese frosting should be thicker and more stable than buttercream. Use enough sugar to achieve this consistency.) If the frosting is too thick, thin it with the milk. If the frosting is too thin, add more powdered sugar, 1 tablespoon at a time, until thickened.

5. Spread the frosting evenly over the cake.

Lighten-up tip: Lower the glycemic index of the batter by replacing 1 cup granulated sugar with ¾ cup pure maple syrup and reducing the amount of oil by ¼ cup.

Technique tip: Not all cakes rise evenly and smoothly, and its normal for your cake to have a dome-shaped top. For stacking and frosting cakes, it's easier if they're flat or leveled. Once your cakes have cooled, place each on a flat surface and run a serrated knife horizontally across the top to shave off any bulges before assembling.

Double Chocolate Torte

PREP TIME: 30 minutes · **COOK TIME:** 30 minutes · **INACTIVE TIME:** 5½ hours

NUT-FREE, SOY-FREE · SERVES: 12

This rich, decadent, showstopping dessert is actually very easy to make. It requires some extended refrigeration time, which helps the cake maintain a firm structure, so plan to make it a day ahead and assemble it just before serving. Traditionally tortes are denser than cakes because they rely on mostly flourless recipes and either a nut or bread crumb base to hold it together. I've lightened this one (and made it nut-free) by swapping out the traditional torte for devil's food cake, which is full of deep chocolate flavor.

FOR THE TORTE

1 cup vegan butter, melted, plus more for greasing

3 cups all-purpose flour, plus more for dusting

2 cups dairy-free semisweet chocolate chips

2 cups granulated sugar

1 cup Dutch-process cocoa powder

2 tablespoons instant coffee

2 teaspoons baking powder

1 teaspoon baking soda

1 cup unsweetened applesauce

1 cup unsweetened coconut yogurt

1 cup hot water

1. Preheat the oven to 350°F. Grease and flour 2 (9-inch) round cake pans.

2. **Make the torte:** In a food processor, process the chocolate chips and sugar until the chips are finely chopped. Transfer to a large bowl. Add the flour, cocoa powder, instant coffee, baking powder, and baking soda.

3. Add the applesauce, yogurt, water, and butter. Whisk until smooth. Divide the batter evenly between the prepared pans.

4. Bake for 25 to 30 minutes, or until a toothpick inserted in the center comes out clean. Remove from the oven. Let cool completely before removing from the pans, about 1½ hours.

FOR THE FROSTING

1 cup vegan cream cheese, at room temperature

1 cup Dutch-process cocoa powder

⅓ cup granulated sugar

1 teaspoon vanilla extract

⅛ teaspoon salt

2 cups Coconut Whipped Cream (page 115) or store-bought

2 tablespoons grated dairy-free 70% dark chocolate, for garnish

5. **Make the frosting:** Using an electric hand mixer in a large bowl, beat the cream cheese, cocoa powder, sugar, vanilla, and salt on medium-high until smooth. Fold in the whipped cream.

6. Cut the cakes in half lengthwise so that you have 4 layers. Put 1 layer on a cake dish, and add ¼ of the frosting. Top with another layer of cake. Repeat until all 4 cake layers are stacked and the top layer is frosted on top. Garnish with the dark chocolate. Refrigerate for at least 4 hours before serving.

Make-ahead tip: Bake your cakes according to the instructions, let cool completely at room temperature, then wrap them in plastic wrap and refrigerate overnight. Remove the cakes from the refrigerator, slice in half, and build your torte just before you're ready to serve it.

Toasted Coconut Layer Cake

PREP TIME: 20 minutes · **COOK TIME:** 50 minutes · **INACTIVE TIME:** 30 minutes

NUT-FREE, SOY-FREE · **SERVES:** 12 to 16

This toasted coconut cake is a wonderful switch from classic vanilla or white birthday cake. Toasting the coconut brings out its natural sweetness and adds an almost marshmallow-like taste to the frosting. This recipe is nut-free, but if nuts aren't an issue, adding a half teaspoon of almond extract to the cake batter and the frosting adds another level of depth. Choose a natural almond extract and don't add more than a teaspoon—almond extract can be overpowering and bitter if you use too much.

FOR THE CAKE

¾ cup vegan butter, at room temperature, plus more for greasing

1½ cups shredded unsweetened coconut

1 (5-ounce) can coconut milk

1 tablespoon apple cider vinegar

3 cups all-purpose flour

2 teaspoons baking powder

½ teaspoon baking soda

½ teaspoon salt

1½ cups granulated sugar

1 cup unsweetened applesauce

1 teaspoon vanilla extract

1 teaspoon coconut extract

1. Preheat the oven to 350°F. Line a small rimmed baking sheet with parchment paper. Grease 2 (9-inch) round cake pans, then line the bottoms with parchment paper and grease again.

2. **Make the cake:** Place the shredded coconut in a single layer on the prepared baking sheet. Bake, watching closely to avoid burning, for about 5 minutes, or until lightly toasted. Remove from the oven. Let cool completely.

3. In a 4-cup glass measuring cup, combine the milk and vinegar. Let stand for 5 minutes.

4. In a large bowl, whisk the flour, baking powder, baking soda, and salt. Using an electric hand mixer in another large bowl, cream together the sugar and butter on medium-high for about 5 minutes, or until light and fluffy. Add the applesauce, vanilla, and coconut extract. Mix until combined.

5. Reduce the mixer speed to low. Starting and ending with the dry ingredients, alternate adding the dry ingredients and milk mixture, scraping down the bowl between each addition. Gently fold in ½ cup of toasted coconut.

FOR THE FROSTING

2 cups vegan butter, at
   room temperature
6 cups powdered sugar
1 teaspoon vanilla extract
1 teaspoon
   coconut extract

6. Divide the batter evenly between the pre-pared pans and bake for 40 to 45 minutes, or until a toothpick inserted in the center comes out clean. Remove from the oven. Let cool for 30 minutes, then transfer to a wire rack to finish cooling.

7. **Make the frosting:** Using an electric hand mixer in a large bowl, beat the butter on medium-high until pale and creamy. Reduce the speed to medium and add the sugar, ½ cup at a time, mixing well between each addition. Add the vanilla, coconut extract, and ½ cup of toasted coconut. Mix until combined.

8. Level off the tops of the cakes (see technique tip on page 53), then put 1 cake layer on a plate. Add ⅓ of the frosting and smooth into an even layer covering the cake. Place the remaining cake on top followed by the remaining frosting. Using an offset spatula, smooth the frosting down the sides to frost the entire cake. Sprinkle the remaining ½ cup of toasted coconut on top.

Lighten-up tip: Replace the ¾ cup butter in the batter with a coconut-based dairy-free Greek yogurt, such as Daiya brand. You can use plain or vanilla (but flavored ones will have more sugar).

Technique tip: Show off your cake-making skills: Slice each layer in half lengthwise to create a 4-layer cake. Double the frosting recipe and the amount of toasted coconut and alternate a thick layer of frosting and a thin layer of frosting between the cakes, following the instructions in step 8. It'll look beautiful when sliced and add even more toasted coconut flavor.

Black Forest Cake

PREP TIME: 30 minutes · **COOK TIME:** 35 minutes · **INACTIVE TIME:** 4 hours 20 minutes

KID-FRIENDLY, SOY-FREE · **SERVES:** 10 to 12

As a kid in the 1980s, I thought that black forest cake was one of the most chic and sophisticated desserts ever. It was everywhere back then! I'd forgotten about it until my husband asked for a vegan version for his birthday a few years ago. Traditionally, this cake is made with dark chocolate cake, fresh or canned sweet cherries soaked in a cherry liqueur, whipped cream, and chocolate shavings. However, in the interest of keeping this cake kid-friendly and less time-consuming, cherry pie filling and almond extract replace the alcohol-soaked fruit. I do recommend making the cakes ahead of time, since they require extensive chilling to set up properly.

FOR THE CAKE
½ cup canola oil, plus more for greasing
⅔ cup Dutch-process cocoa powder, plus more for dusting
1 cup unsweetened almond milk
1 tablespoon fresh lemon juice
1¾ cups all-purpose flour
2 teaspoons baking soda
1 teaspoon baking powder
1 teaspoon salt
1½ cups granulated sugar
1 cup brewed coffee, hot
½ cup unsweetened applesauce
2 teaspoons vanilla extract

1. Preheat the oven to 350°F. Grease the bottom and sides of 2 (9-inch) round cake pans and dust with cocoa powder.

2. **Make the cake:** In a glass measuring cup, combine the milk and lemon juice. Let stand for about 5 minutes.

3. In a large bowl, whisk the flour, cocoa powder, baking soda, baking powder, and salt.

4. In a medium bowl, combine the sugar, milk mixture, coffee, applesauce, oil, and vanilla. Whisk until a smooth but thin batter forms. Divide evenly between the prepared cake pans, smoothing out the tops, and bake for 30 to 35 minutes, or until a toothpick inserted in the center comes out clean. Remove from the oven. Let cool for 15 minutes, then transfer to wire racks to cool completely. Cover in plastic wrap and refrigerate for at least 4 hours (up to overnight).

FOR THE FILLING

1 (21-ounce) can cherry
   pie filling
1 tablespoon
   almond extract

FOR THE TOPPINGS

2 recipes Coconut
   Whipped Cream
   (page 115), chilled or
   1 (8-ounce) container
   store-bought
Fresh or canned dark
   sweet cherries, for
   garnish (optional)
2 cups grated dairy-free
   70% dark chocolate, for
   garnish (optional)

5. **Make the filling:** In a medium bowl, combine the pie filling and almond extract.

6. Slice the cakes in half horizontally. Place 1 layer on a cake pedestal or plate. Add a thin layer of whipped cream and top with half of the filling. Top with another layer of cake and a thick layer (about ½ inch) of whipped cream. Add another layer of cake and top with the remaining filling. Place the last layer of cake on top and use the remaining whipped cream. Garnish with cherries (if using) and the chocolate (if using).

Lighten-up tip: In the batter, replace ½ cup sugar with mashed banana. It adds richness to the chocolate flavor.

Deeply Delish Frosted Chocolate Cake

PREP TIME: 25 minutes · **COOK TIME:** 40 minutes · **INACTIVE TIME:** 3 hours 10 minutes

KID-FRIENDLY, NUT-FREE, SOY-FREE · SERVES: 9

In my pre-vegan days, I had a brief but very intense fling with an iconic Canadian frozen chocolate dessert: the McCain Deep'n Delicious cake. I hadn't had one in years but would still have a pang of jealousy whenever a friend would eat one. Until now. This copycat frozen sheet cake is moist and fluffy and has a similar whipped, fudgy frosting. Like its grocery-store counterpart, this cake is best when eaten half-frozen.

FOR THE CAKE

5 tablespoons vegetable oil, plus more for greasing
1½ cups all-purpose flour
1 cup granulated sugar
¼ cup Dutch-process cocoa powder, plus more for dusting
1 teaspoon baking soda
½ teaspoon salt
1 cup water
1 teaspoon white vinegar
1 teaspoon vanilla extract

FOR THE FROSTING

Vegetable oil, for greasing
2 cups dairy-free semisweet chocolate chips
1 (14-ounce) can condensed coconut milk
1 teaspoon vanilla extract
½ cup chocolate syrup, plus more as needed
¼ cup vegan chocolate sprinkles, for garnish

1. Preheat the oven to 350°F. Grease an 8-by-8-inch baking pan.

2. **Make the cake:** In a large bowl, combine the flour, sugar, cocoa powder, baking soda, and salt. Add the water, oil, vinegar, and vanilla. Stir until no lumps remain.

3. Pour into the prepared pan and bake for 30 to 35 minutes, or until a toothpick inserted in the center comes out clean. Remove from the oven. Let cool for 10 minutes, then refrigerate for 1 hour.

4. **Make the frosting:** Grease an 8-by-8-inch baking pan and line with parchment paper.

5. In a heat-proof glass bowl set over a pot filled with 2 to 3 inches of simmering water, heat the chocolate chips and condensed milk, stirring frequently, for about 5 minutes, or until the chocolate chips have melted and fully mixed with the milk. Stir in the vanilla.

6. Transfer to the prepared pan and refrigerate for about 2 hours, or until completely cooled.

7. Using an electric hand mixer in a large bowl, whip the cooled frosting mix and chocolate syrup on medium-high for 5 to 10 minutes, or until fluffy. If the frosting is still too thick, add more syrup, 1 tablespoon at a time.

8. Transfer the frosting to a piping bag fitted with a large star tip and pipe icing rosettes in rows until the cake is covered, or frost the cake completely using an offset spatula. Garnish with the sprinkles. Refrigerate until serving.

Ingredient tip: Although many of these recipes call for melting chocolate in the microwave, I don't recommend it here, since the condensed coconut milk can easily burn (and make a huge mess!).

Lighten-up tip: Swap the frosting with my healthier chocolate-avocado version in the lighten-up tip on page 43. It cuts down on sugar and saves time, since there's no refrigeration or setting required.

4

PIES, PASTRIES, AND TARTS

← ⚓

Date-Caramel Banoffee Pie

Coconut Cream Mini Tarts

PREP TIME: 10 minutes · **COOK TIME:** 5 minutes

BIG BATCH, KID-FRIENDLY, NUT-FREE · MAKES: 30 mini tarts

These little tarts are the star of any get-together. They look like they took hours to make, but they come together in minutes, thanks to the use of some fantastic store-bought ingredients. Mini phyllo tart cups give this dessert a nice switch from traditional piecrust and work well to contain the delicious filling.

2 (15-pack) packages frozen mini vegan phyllo tart shells, such as Fillo Factory brand

1½ cups shredded sweetened coconut

2 (3.4-ounce) packages vegan instant vanilla pudding mix

2 (15-ounce) cans coconut milk, refrigerated overnight

2 cups Coconut Whipped Cream (page 115) or store-bought

1. Preheat the oven to 350°F.

2. Put the tart shells on a rimmed baking sheet. Line another baking sheet with parchment paper, and put the shredded coconut on it. Bake the tart shells for 3 to 5 minutes. Toast the coconut for 3 to 4 minutes, or until lightly golden. Remove both from the oven.

3. Using an electric hand mixer in a medium bowl, whisk the instant pudding mix and milk on medium until thickened.

4. Scoop the pudding into the shells. Top with the whipped cream and toasted coconut.

Variation tip: Make these into chocolate-coconut mini tarts by swapping out 1 package instant vanilla pudding for instant chocolate pudding. Shave a little dark chocolate on top with the toasted coconut. If you can't find vegan phyllo tart shells, you can make this recipe using my No-Fail Piecrust (page 108). Cut the dough to fill the cups of a muffin tin, use a fork to poke holes in the bottom of the crust (to keep it from rising), bake at 375°F for about 10 minutes, then cool.

Ginger-Pear Pie Bites

PREP TIME: 15 minutes · **COOK TIME:** 15 minutes

KID-FRIENDLY, SOY-FREE · MAKES: 8 pie bites

Crescent rolls are a great staple to keep in your refrigerator for quick and easy desserts that are fun to eat. I like making these with my kids because they take very little time (just 30 minutes start to finish), and they get little hands working in the kitchen. Try these with a variety of different fillings for a sweet treat in any season!

¼ cup packed brown sugar

⅓ cup chopped pecans or walnuts (optional)

1 teaspoon ground cinnamon

½ teaspoon ground ginger

¼ teaspoon ground nutmeg

4 tablespoons vegan butter, melted, divided

1 (8-ounce) can crescent rolls

1 large ripe Anjou or Bartlett pear, cut into 8 slices

1. Preheat the oven to 350°F. Line a rimmed baking sheet with parchment paper.

2. In a small bowl, combine the sugar, pecans (if using), cinnamon, ginger, and nutmeg. Pour in 3 tablespoons of butter and stir until mixed.

3. Unwrap the rolls and put the dough on the prepared baking sheet. Spread the sugar mixture evenly on each roll. Place 1 pear slice at the wide end of each roll and roll up to form a crescent.

4. Brush the tops with the remaining 1 tablespoon of butter and bake for 10 to 12 minutes, or until golden brown.

Variation tip: Apples work really well in this recipe for a quick apple pie bite. Or swap in fresh peaches when in season. My kids also like using bananas and chocolate chips.

Ingredient tip: As hard as it might be to believe, Pillsbury Crescent Rolls don't contain any dairy or eggs.

Canadian Butter Tarts

PREP TIME: 45 minutes · **COOK TIME:** 30 minutes · **INACTIVE TIME:** 50 minutes

BIG BATCH, NUT-FREE, SOY-FREE · MAKES: 12 tarts

I'm Canadian, and there isn't a dessert that says "Canada" more than a good old-fashioned butter tart. The good news is that you don't have to live north of the 49th parallel to enjoy this treat! Butter tarts are a fantastic way to shake up any potluck, bake sale, or brunch. To make the dough you use a mix of both vegan butter and vegetable shortening: butter because it adds flavor and flakiness, and shortening to give the dough a bit more structure—which you'll need to hold in all the buttery, syrupy filling.

FOR THE CRUST

2½ cups all-purpose
   flour, plus more
   for dusting
¼ cup granulated sugar
½ teaspoon salt
½ cup vegan butter,
   cold, plus more
   for greasing
½ cup vegetable
   shortening
½ cup ice water

FOR THE FILLING

¼ cup hot water
2 tablespoons ground
   flaxseed
¾ cup packed
   brown sugar
½ cup maple syrup
½ cup vegan
   butter, melted
3 tablespoons cornstarch
1 teaspoon white vinegar
¼ teaspoon salt
¾ cup soft
   seedless raisins

1. **Make the crust:** In a large bowl, combine the flour, sugar, and salt. Using a pastry cutter, cut the butter and shortening into the flour until it resembles coarse cornmeal. (If you don't have a pastry cutter, use 2 knives, cutting in criss-cross motions.) Add the water, 2 tablespoons at a time, until a loose dough forms.

2. Bring the dough together into a disc, wrap in plastic wrap, and refrigerate for 30 minutes.

3. Preheat the oven to 350°F. Grease a standard muffin tin.

4. On a lightly floured surface, roll out the dough to about ¼-inch thickness. Using a 6-inch-diameter bowl, cut the dough into circles and stuff into each muffin cup, pressing down to form a bottom and letting the excess cover the sides. Bake for 5 minutes, or until cooked. Remove from the oven and let cool slightly.

5. **Make the filling:** In a small bowl, combine the water and flaxseed. Let stand for about 5 minutes.

6. In a large bowl, combine the sugar, maple syrup, butter, flaxseed mixture, cornstarch, vinegar, and salt. Using an electric hand mixer, beat on medium until smooth.

7. Divide the raisins evenly among the tart shells, then fill each about ¾ full with the filling. Bake for 20 to 25 minutes, or until the filling has set and the pastry is golden brown. Remove from the oven. Let cool for 15 minutes, then remove from the tin and let cool completely on a wire rack.

Variation tip: Classic Canadian butter tarts contain raisins in the filling, but if you're like me and not a fan of raisins in your desserts, simply omit them or swap them out for pecans.

Ingredient tip: If your raisins aren't soft, just soak them in warm water for 15 minutes before using.

Easy Summer Peach and Berry Cobbler

PREP TIME: 15 minutes · **COOK TIME:** 45 minutes

BIG BATCH, NUT-FREE · SERVES: 12 to 16

This is an easy, breezy dessert that is always a crowd-pleaser. It takes only minutes to assemble and then the oven does all the work so you don't have to. In the summer, when fresh berries are plentiful, I like to grab a mix of blueberries, blackberries, and raspberries and pair them with fresh peaches to fill this dish. Their striking colors and sweet-tart flavors are a perfect pairing for the doughy, rich cobbler topping.

FOR THE COBBLER

½ cup vegan butter, cold, plus more for greasing

1 pint fresh blueberries

1 pint fresh raspberries

2 cups diced fresh peaches (about 3 peaches)

½ pint fresh blackberries

2 tablespoons plus ½ cup granulated sugar, divided

2 teaspoons lemon zest

2 cups all-purpose flour

Scant ¼ cup baking powder

1 teaspoon salt

1 cup unsweetened soy milk

FOR THE TOPPING

⅔ cup granulated sugar

¼ cup cornstarch

1½ cups boiling water

1. Preheat the oven to 350°F. Grease a 9-by-13-inch baking pan.

2. **Make the cobbler:** In the prepared baking pan, toss the blueberries, raspberries, peaches, blackberries, 2 tablespoons of sugar, and the zest to combine, then spread evenly.

3. In a large bowl, combine the flour, remaining ½ cup of sugar, the baking powder, and salt. Using a pastry cutter, cut the butter into the mixture. (If you don't have a pastry cutter, use 2 knives, cutting in criss-cross motions.) Stir in the milk to form loose dough. Spoon over the fruit.

4. **Make the topping:** In a small bowl, combine the sugar and cornstarch. Sprinkle over the dough. Pour the water over the entire dish. Bake for 40 to 45 minutes, or until the fruit is tender and bubbling. Remove from the oven.

Variation tip: If fresh berries aren't in season, swap them out for 6 cups frozen berry blend (no need to thaw beforehand!).

Mini Dark Chocolate and Caramel Tarts

PREP TIME: 20 minutes • **COOK TIME:** 15 minutes • **INACTIVE TIME:** 2 hours 20 minutes

NUT-FREE, SOY-FREE • **MAKES:** 12 mini tarts

These little tarts are rich and decadent, yet deceptively easy to make. The filling is a quick caramel sauce that doesn't require a candy thermometer and comes together in a few minutes. Level up these tarts by adding a dollop of dairy-free whipped cream and a fresh raspberry or two on top before serving.

FOR THE CRUST

¼ cup plus 2 tablespoons vegan butter, melted, plus more for greasing

2 cups crushed vegan shortbread cookies

½ cup granulated sugar

FOR THE FILLING

1 cup granulated sugar

½ cup water

1½ cups coconut cream, divided

1¼ teaspoons sea salt, divided

1¼ cups dairy-free 70% dark chocolate, chopped

2 teaspoons coconut oil

1. Preheat the oven to 350°F. Grease a standard muffin tin.

2. **Make the crust:** In a large bowl, combine the cookies, sugar, and butter. Divide evenly into the prepared muffin tin, pressing firmly into the bottoms and sides. Bake for 10 minutes, or until lightly golden. Remove from the oven, and let cool to room temperature.

3. **Make the filling:** In a small saucepan, bring the sugar and water to a boil without stirring. Continue boiling for 5 to 10 minutes, or just until light amber. Remove from the heat. Slowly pour in 1 cup of coconut cream (the mixture will bubble) and ¾ teaspoon of salt. Mix until smooth.

4. Pour into the tart shells and refrigerate for about 20 minutes, or until the caramel is firm.

5. In a pot, bring the remaining ½ cup of coconut cream just to a boil. Add the chocolate and stir until smooth. Add the oil and ¼ teaspoon of salt. Stir until glossy. Pour over the chilled tarts and refrigerate for about 2 hours, or until firm. Sprinkle with the remaining ¼ teaspoon of salt.

Ingredient tip: I like using Lotus Biscoff cookies, which are a delicate spiced shortbread cookie that have a naturally caramel-like flavor. If you don't have Biscoff cookies, you can use any vegan shortbread-style cookie for the crust.

Mile-High Lemon Meringue Pie

PREP TIME: 30 minutes · **COOK TIME:** 25 to 30 minutes
INACTIVE TIME: 2 hours 20 minutes

NUT-FREE, SOY-FREE · SERVES: 8

If you haven't experienced vegan meringue, prepare to have your mind blown.
We're talking fluffy, marshmallow-y meringue, all without the use of eggs. This
recipe uses my basic meringue that, once mastered, can be used to top a lemon
meringue (or Key lime) pie or baked into chewy meringue cookies or a pavlova. If
you have a small kitchen blowtorch, you can use it to toast the outer shell of the
meringue. If not, a couple of minutes under your oven's broiler works just as well.

1 recipe No-Fail Piecrust
  (page 108) or
  store-bought
1½ cups granulated sugar
1¼ cups full-fat
  coconut milk
¾ cup fresh lemon juice
  (about 4 to 5 lemons)
5 tablespoons cornstarch
2 teaspoons lemon zest
1 recipe Eggless
  Meringue (page 109)

1. Preheat the oven to 375°F.

2. Roll out the piecrust between ½- and ¼-inch
   thick. Transfer to 9-inch pie dish, pressing
   down on the bottom and sides. Trim away
   any excess crust. Use a fork to poke holes all
   over the bottom and sides and bake for about
   10 minutes, or until golden. Remove from
   the oven.

3. Meanwhile, in a medium saucepan over medium
   heat, combine the sugar, milk, lemon juice,
   cornstarch, and zest. Whisk well to ensure
   the cornstarch is fully dissolved. Cook, stirring
   constantly, for 5 to 6 minutes, or until the sugar
   is fully dissolved and the mixture has thickened
   into a loose curd-like consistency. Once it starts
   to thicken, it will do so quickly.

4. Spread evenly over the crust and bake for
   15 minutes, or until the filling is just bubbling
   around the edges. Remove from the oven, let
   cool for 15 to 20 minutes, then refrigerate for at
   least 2 hours to set.

5. Spread the meringue on top, using a spatula to
   form giant peaks. Place under a broiler, watching carefully to not burn it, for 1 to 2 minutes, or
   until the peaks are browned. Let cool.

Grandma's Blueberry Pie

PREP TIME: 15 minutes · **COOK TIME:** 50 minutes

NUT-FREE, SOY-FREE · SERVES: 8

This is the ultimate summertime pie. Fresh blueberries are at their best from May to late September, depending on your location, and this pie is a great way to show them off. Feel free to experiment with different style tops for this pie, like a lattice crust, or cut the dough into shapes using cookie cutters and lay on top of the filled pie.

All-purpose flour,
  for dusting
2 recipes No-Fail Piecrust
  (page 108), divided
4 cups fresh blueberries
¾ cup granulated sugar
3 tablespoons cornstarch
1 tablespoon fresh
  lemon juice
½ teaspoon ground
  cinnamon
½ teaspoon lemon zest
¼ teaspoon salt
2 tablespoons water
  (optional)
1 tablespoon coarse
  sugar (optional)

1. Preheat the oven to 375°F. On a floured surface, roll out 1 piecrust into a ⅛-inch-thick circle and transfer to a 9-inch pie dish, trimming off any excess dough.

2. In a large bowl, toss the blueberries, granulated sugar, cornstarch, lemon juice, cinnamon, zest, and salt to combine. Transfer to the pie dish.

3. On a floured surface, roll out the 1 remaining piecrust into a ⅛-inch-thick circle. Place on top of the pie, using your thumbs or a fork to crimp the edges shut. Cut an X-shaped slit in the top to vent steam.

4. Brush with water (if using) and sprinkle with coarse sugar (if using) for a classic bakery-style texture. Bake for 50 minutes, or until the crust is golden brown.

Time-saving tip: No time to make and chill pie dough? Grab a store-bought vegan pie shell and make an open-faced version of this pie.

Date-Caramel Banoffee Pie

PREP TIME: 45 minutes · **INACTIVE TIME:** 1 hour 30 minutes

SERVES: 12

Banoffee pie is a fun English dessert that combines sticky toffee or caramel with bananas and whipped cream and sometimes chocolate. It's typically made on a cookie crumb base but can also be made with crushed Graham crackers or a traditional piecrust (if you feel like being extra). I've harnessed the power of Medjool dates to create a naturally sweet caramel filling for this version and used a store-bought dairy-free whipped cream. I prefer Lotus Biscoff cookies for this recipe because they have a great cinnamon-spice flavor that's a nice contrast to the sweetness of the pie, but any vegan shortbread cookie will be delicious.

2 cups pitted Medjool dates

1 (8.8-ounce) package vegan shortbread cookies

¼ cup vegan butter, melted

¾ cup unsweetened almond milk

1 teaspoon vanilla extract

¼ teaspoon salt

2 large bananas, sliced

1 (9-ounce) container frozen coconut whipped cream, thawed

¼ cup shaved dairy-free 70% dark chocolate, for garnish

1. Put the dates in a bowl filled with warm water and soak for 30 minutes. Drain.

2. Meanwhile, in a food processor, pulse the cookies until they reach a crumb consistency. Transfer to a bowl and add the butter. Stir with a fork until mixed.

3. Pour into a 9-inch springform or removable-bottom tart pan. Using the bottom of a glass, press the crumbs firmly into the pan bottom, creating a crust. Refrigerate while you make the filling.

4. In the food processor, combine the dates, milk, vanilla, and salt. Pulse until smooth.

5. Spread the date-caramel filling into an even layer in the crust. Top with a single layer of bananas and a layer of whipped cream, and then top with the remaining banana slices.

6. Sprinkle with the chocolate. Refrigerate for 1 hour before serving.

Strawberry Custard Napoleons

PREP TIME: 10 minutes · **COOK TIME:** 20 minutes · **INACTIVE TIME:** 4 hours

SERVES: 8

Napoleons, or *mille-feuille* ("one thousand layers"), are a light yet rich French dessert made from layers of flaky puff pastry, creamy vanilla custard, and powdered sugar. My aunt is French-Canadian and makes just about the best mille-feuille ever. I've done my best to replicate her recipe with vegan ingredients. Traditionally, this dish is strictly pastry and custard—which, in this recipe, can be prepared beforehand or while you bake and cool the puff pastry—but I've added a layer of fresh strawberries to brighten it up and cut some of the richness.

1 sheet vegan puff pastry, such as Pepperidge Farm brand, thawed

1 recipe Vanilla Custard (page 114)

1 pint fresh strawberries, sliced

3 tablespoons powdered sugar, for dusting

1. Preheat the oven to 400°F.

2. Roll out the puff pastry to fit a rimmed baking sheet and cut in half lengthwise. Use a fork to poke holes throughout. Bake for 15 to 20 minutes. Remove from the oven. Let cool completely.

3. Carefully separate the top and bottom of both slices of cooked puff pastry (or cut in half). Place the bottoms on a long platter or baking pan.

4. Divide the custard between both bottom pieces, spreading out evenly. Add a single layer of strawberries and top with the remaining sheets of puff pastry. Refrigerate for 4 hours to set. Dust with the sugar before slicing with a serrated knife and serving.

Technique tip: For a double-decker Napoleon: Use 1½ sheets of puff pastry and double the vanilla custard recipe. Bake 3 half sheets of puff pastry according to the directions above. When cooled, cut in half. Use 2 pieces of puff pastry as the base. Repeat the layering process in step 4 twice, until all ingredients are used, and then refrigerate and garnish as directed.

Tiramisu

PREP TIME: 1 hour · **COOK TIME:** 25 minutes · **INACTIVE TIME:** 2 hours

SOY-FREE · SERVES: 12 to 16

This classic Italian dessert is my all-time favorite treat, so I'm excited to share this easy vegan adaptation. I use a vanilla sheet cake since most ladyfinger cookies aren't vegan and baking your own is quite a process, and I've omitted the coffee liqueur, but the result is no less delicious.

2 cups all-purpose flour

1½ cups granulated sugar

1¼ teaspoons
    salt, divided

1 teaspoon
    baking powder

¼ teaspoon baking soda

½ cup vegetable oil

½ cup unsweetened
    coconut yogurt

1 teaspoon
    almond extract

1 cup vegan butter

1 cup water

1½ cups raw cashews

½ cup maple syrup

⅓ cup coconut
    oil, melted

½ cup unsweetened
    almond milk

1 teaspoon vanilla extract

2 cups Coconut Whipped
    Cream (page 115) or
    store-bought

1 cup strong brewed
    coffee, at room
    temperature, divided

1. Preheat the oven to 375°F. Line a 10-by-15-inch rimmed baking sheet with parchment paper, leaving extra hanging over the edges.

2. In a large bowl, combine the flour, sugar, 1 teaspoon of salt, the baking powder, and baking soda. In a small bowl, whisk the vegetable oil, yogurt, and almond extract.

3. In a small saucepan, bring the butter and water to just under a boil. Stir into the flour mixture, then add the yogurt mixture and whisk until fully blended.

4. Pour into the prepared baking sheet and bake for 18 to 22 minutes, or until a toothpick inserted in the center comes out clean and the top is golden. Remove from the oven. Let cool completely.

5. In a high-speed blender, blend the cashews, maple syrup, coconut oil, milk, vanilla, and the remaining ¼ teaspoon of salt until creamy. Transfer to a bowl and fold in the whipped cream.

FOR DECORATING

2 tablespoons
  cocoa powder

¼ cup shaved dairy-free
  70% dark chocolate

6. Cut the cake in half, then trim to fit in an 8-by-8-inch baking pan. Place 1 layer of cake on the bottom and pour ½ cup of coffee on top. Top with half of the cashew filling, spreading out with an offset spatula.

7. Place the other half of the cake on top. Pour the remaining ½ cup of coffee on top of the cake, and then top with the remaining cashew filling.

8. Spread the filling evenly across the cake. Dust with the cocoa powder and garnish with the chocolate shavings. Refrigerate for at least 2 hours before cutting and serving.

Time-saving tip: Don't feel like making a cake from scratch? You can swap out my vanilla sheet cake recipe for a box of Duncan Hines classic white cake. Prepare the recipe according to the package instructions for a 9-by-13-inch pan, swapping out the eggs for ¼ cup applesauce per egg. Then proceed with the recipe starting with step 5.

Variation tip: If you have a bottle of coffee liqueur lying around, swap out half of the brewed coffee for it.

SPOON DESSERTS

Rainbow Sherbet 78	Espresso Crème Caramel 84
Frozen Chocolate- Peppermint Mousse Pots 79	Caramelized Banana- Pecan Parfait 86
No-Churn Rocky Road Ice Cream 80	Blackberry Eton Mess 87
Triple Pudding Parfait 81	Raspberry Chocolate Trifle 88
Chocolate Mousse 83	

←—◁

Blackberry Eton Mess

Rainbow Sherbet

PREP TIME: 10 minutes · **INACTIVE TIME:** 4 hours

BIG BATCH, GLUTEN-FREE, KID-FRIENDLY, NUT-FREE, SOY-FREE · **SERVES:** 12

As a kid, was there anything more fun and refreshing than getting a scoop (or two) of fruity rainbow sherbet? The flavor combination of raspberry, orange, and lemon-lime is forever etched in my mind as a classic summer treat. Since most sherbet contains milk, egg whites, or gelatin, I created a vegan version to cool off with when the temperatures climb. Note that you'll need a high-speed blender or food processor and airtight freezer-safe containers. You can serve this frozen treat immediately as soft-serve or freeze it for 3 to 4 hours for a more traditional ice cream.

3 (14-ounce) cans sweetened condensed coconut milk, divided

4 cups frozen raspberries

2 cups frozen peaches

2 cups frozen mango

2 cups ice cubes

⅓ cup granulated sugar

2 tablespoons fresh lemon juice

2 tablespoons fresh lime juice

1 teaspoon lemon zest

1 teaspoon lime zest

1. In a high-speed blender or food processor, blend 1 can of condensed milk and the raspberries until creamy. Transfer to an airtight, freezer-safe container and freeze for 3 to 4 hours.

2. Blend 1 can of condensed milk, the peaches, and mango until creamy. Transfer to an airtight, freezer-safe container and freeze for 3 to 4 hours.

3. In a medium bowl, combine the remaining 1 can of condensed milk, the ice cubes, sugar, lemon juice, lime juice, lemon zest, and lime zest. Whisk until smooth and the sugar is dissolved. Transfer to an airtight, freezer-safe container and freeze for 3 to 4 hours.

4. Place one scoopful of each flavor into a bowl or cone.

Lighten-up tip: Since the lime sherbet is the only flavor that contains refined sugar, you can replace it with another fruit, like cherry or blackberry.

Variation tip: This recipe is basically a 14-ounce can sweetened condensed coconut milk and about 4 cups of your favorite fruit (or fruit combinations). Try mixing this up to create your own favorite flavors.

Frozen Chocolate-Peppermint Mousse Pots

PREP TIME: 25 minutes · **INACTIVE TIME:** 2 hours 20 minutes

GLUTEN-FREE, KID-FRIENDLY · SERVES: 4

Rich, creamy, and crunchy, these chocolate-peppermint pots are like frozen Peppermint Patties on a spoon. They're perfectly delicious served as a mousse but are even better when they have the chance to freeze. While this version is a fun treat to serve the entire family, you can easily turn this into an adults-only dessert by swapping out the almond extract for 2 tablespoons dark rum. The rum adds a great caramel flavor that pairs well with dark chocolate.

1½ cups dairy-free dark chocolate chips

2 (16-ounce) packages silken tofu, drained

¼ cup plus 2 tablespoons maple syrup

2 tablespoons chocolate syrup

1 teaspoon vanilla extract

½ teaspoon almond extract

½ teaspoon salt

6 to 8 red and white peppermint candies, crushed

1. In a heat-proof glass bowl set over a pot filled with 2 to 3 inches of simmering water, heat the chocolate chips, stirring frequently, until melted. (Or melt in the microwave in 30-second intervals until combined and smooth, stirring in between.)

2. In a food processor, process the tofu for 2 minutes, or until smooth. Add the melted chocolate, maple syrup, chocolate syrup, vanilla, almond extract, and salt. Process for about 3 minutes, or until creamy.

3. Evenly divide among 4 freezer-safe cups. Top each with the candies and freeze for 2 hours. Remove from the freezer and thaw for 20 minutes before serving.

Variation tip: I use chocolate chips for this recipe, but you can use the same amount of your favorite dairy-free dark chocolate bar that's around 70% cocoa, since anything higher will be too bitter.

No-Churn Rocky Road Ice Cream

PREP TIME: 15 minutes · **COOK TIME:** 5 minutes · **INACTIVE TIME:** 6 hours 15 minutes

KID-FRIENDLY, SOY-FREE · SERVES: 3 to 4

This isn't your average rocky road ice cream. It's rocky road amped up—and vegan! Rich, creamy, sweet, and salty all in one perfect scoop. The base is frozen banana, which, when pulsed or pureed, creates a luscious frozen treat that doesn't require any churning or a fancy ice cream machine. Serve this straight out of the food processor for a delicious soft-serve treat, or freeze it in an airtight container for 4 to 6 hours to turn it into traditional hard ice cream.

½ cup shredded unsweetened coconut

3 sliced and frozen bananas

½ cup sweetened condensed coconut milk

3 tablespoons Dutch-process cocoa powder

2 tablespoons maple syrup or agave nectar

1 teaspoon vanilla extract

¼ cup dairy-free mini chocolate chips

¼ cup chopped, unsalted almonds

¼ cup mini vegan marshmallows, such as Dandies brand

¼ cup crushed pretzel bits

1. Preheat the oven to 350°F. Line a small rimmed baking sheet with parchment paper. Spread the shredded coconut in an even layer on the prepared baking sheet. Toast, watching carefully, for about 5 minutes, or until lightly browned. Remove from the oven and let cool completely.

2. In a food processor, pulse the bananas until crumbly. Add the condensed milk, cocoa powder, maple syrup, and vanilla. Process until creamy, stopping to scrape down the bowl as needed.

3. Add the toasted coconut, chocolate chips, almonds, and marshmallows. Pulse until just incorporated. Transfer to a bowl and gently fold in the pretzels.

4. Serve immediately as a soft-serve treat, or transfer to an airtight ice cream container and freeze for 4 to 6 hours. Thaw for 15 minutes before serving.

Variation tip: More a fan of mint chocolate chip? Swap out the cocoa powder, almonds, and marshmallows for 3 drops peppermint extract (go easy since it's really strong!). Or keep the cocoa powder and add some crushed candy canes with the peppermint extract for a fun holiday ice cream!

Triple Pudding Parfait

PREP TIME: 25 minutes · **INACTIVE TIME:** 1 hour

GLUTEN-FREE, KID-FRIENDLY, SOY-FREE · SERVES: 4

This dish may look sophisticated, served in fancy glasses, but it's a kid's dream come true: Layers of dark chocolate, vanilla, and "milk chocolate" pudding, topped with whipped cream and a cherry on top! The chocolate pudding in this recipe uses avocado as the base, but the vanilla is actually instant pudding.

1 (3.4-ounce) box vegan instant vanilla pudding mix

2⅔ cups unsweetened almond milk, cold, divided

2 tablespoons dairy-free chocolate chips

1 ripe medium avocado, pitted and peeled

½ cup plus 1 tablespoon Dutch-process cocoa powder, divided

½ cup packed light brown sugar

1 teaspoon vanilla extract

¼ teaspoon salt

1 cup Coconut Whipped Cream (page 115) or store-bought

4 vegan maraschino or fresh cherries (optional)

1. Using an electric hand mixer in a medium bowl, beat the instant pudding mix and 2 cups of milk on medium for about 2 minutes, or until thickened. Refrigerate while you prepare the dark chocolate pudding.

2. In a heat-proof glass bowl set over a pot filled with 2 to 3 inches of simmering water, heat the chocolate chips, stirring frequently, until melted. (Or melt in the microwave in 30-second intervals until smooth, stirring in between.)

3. In a blender or food processor, blend the remaining ⅔ cup of milk, avocado, ½ cup of cocoa powder, the sugar, melted chocolate, vanilla, and salt until smooth and creamy. Transfer half to a separate bowl and combine with half the vanilla pudding to create a "milk chocolate" layer.

4. Divide the remaining dark chocolate pudding evenly among 4 glasses. Top each with a layer of the remaining vanilla pudding, followed by a layer of the "milk chocolate" pudding. Top each parfait with the whipped cream, a cherry (if using), and a dusting of the remaining 1 tablespoon of cocoa powder. Refrigerate for 1 hour to set.

Variation tip: Add some texture with a layer of chopped roasted peanuts or crushed vegan chocolate sandwich cookies between the chocolate and vanilla pudding.

Chocolate Mousse

PREP TIME: 10 minutes · **INACTIVE TIME:** 1 hour

GLUTEN-FREE, KID-FRIENDLY, NUT-FREE · SERVES: 4

Chocolate mousse is one of those desserts that seems fancy and complicated but couldn't be simpler. The hardest part is waiting for it to chill before eating it! To achieve the velvety consistency of traditional mousse, I use silken tofu, but if you're trying to avoid soy, you can easily swap it out for one to two ripe avocados, depending on their size. This mousse is fabulous in my Raspberry-Chocolate Trifle recipe on page 88 and can also be used as one of the chocolate pudding layers in my Triple Pudding Parfait (page 81) or Chocolate Lasagna (page 102). For a slightly elevated presentation, top the mousse with shaved chocolate.

1 (3½-ounce) bar dairy-free 70% dark chocolate

1 teaspoon coconut oil

1 (12-ounce) package silken tofu

3 tablespoons maple syrup

2 tablespoons Dutch-process cocoa powder

½ teaspoon vanilla extract

¼ teaspoon salt

1. In a heat-proof glass bowl set over a small pot filled with 2 to 3 inches of simmering water, heat the chocolate and oil, stirring frequently, until melted.

2. In a food processor, blend the tofu, melted chocolate, maple syrup, cocoa powder, vanilla, and salt until completely smooth. Transfer to a bowl and refrigerate for 1 hour.

Espresso Crème Caramel

PREP TIME: 15 minutes · **COOK TIME:** 25 minutes · **INACTIVE TIME:** 12 hours or overnight

GLUTEN-FREE, NUT-FREE, SOY-FREE · SERVES: 6

This French-inspired dessert has "wow" written all over it. Traditional recipes consist of a custard made from milk, eggs, and sugar that is topped with a sticky caramel layer. In this veganized version, the custard is egg- and dairy-free, but it's no less delicious. The process might seem intimidating, but it just requires a little patience and a lot of careful watching. The caramel for this dish can burn super fast if you're not vigilant. This dessert needs time to set up, so I definitely recommend making it the day before you plan to serve it. Crème caramel is usually served in 6-ounce ramekins, but if you don't have them on hand, you can divide the mixture among heat-resistant teacups, coffee mugs, or ceramic bowls.

FOR THE CARAMEL

1½ cups superfine
    sugar, divided
½ cup water

FOR THE CUSTARD

2 (14-ounce) cans full-fat
    coconut milk
⅓ cup brewed espresso
    or strong coffee
1¼ teaspoons cornstarch
½ teaspoon
    vanilla extract

1. Set 6 (6-ounce) ramekins on a flat surface.

2. **Make the caramel:** In a medium saucepan, bring the sugar and water to a boil over high heat without stirring. Reduce the heat to a simmer. Cook, watching constantly, for 5 to 10 minutes, or until dark caramel spots start to appear. Pick up the saucepan and swirl 2 or 3 times, then return to the stovetop until the sauce is dark amber. Immediately pour the caramel into the ramekins.

3. **Make the custard:** In a medium saucepan, bring the milk, espresso, cornstarch, and vanilla to a simmer over medium heat. Cook, whisking constantly, for 10 to 15 minutes, or until thickened.

4. Strain the mixture through a fine-mesh sieve to remove any lumps. Pour the custard on top of the caramel. Refrigerate for at least 12 hours (up to overnight).

5. Hold 1 ramekin in your hand, covering the top, and give it a small but firm side-to-side shake. Invert a dessert plate on top of the ramekin and flip the entire thing over so the plate is on the bottom and the ramekin on top. Place the plate on a flat surface and gently lift the ramekin up to remove the dessert. If the crème caramel doesn't turn out onto the plate, try running a knife around the edges to help loosen it. Repeat for the remaining ramekins.

Variation tip: Up for a challenge? Make a crème brûlée. Prepare the custard only, doubling the amount of vanilla and omitting the espresso. Chill as required, then just before serving, top with a thin layer of granulated sugar and use a kitchen torch or oven broiler to gently caramelize it. Make sure your ramekins or cups are heat-proof or oven-safe.

Ingredient tip: To make superfine sugar, put the amount of granulated sugar called for plus 2 extra tablespoons in a food processor and process for 2 minutes. Let sit for 30 seconds and then check for a consistency of fine sand. Continue to pulse in 30-second increments as needed.

Caramelized Banana-Pecan Parfait

PREP TIME: 20 minutes · **COOK TIME:** 20 minutes · **INACTIVE TIME:** 30 minutes

GLUTEN-FREE, KID-FRIENDLY, SOY-FREE · SERVES: 4

This is a fun, no-alcohol-needed take on bananas Foster—bananas cooked in butter, brown sugar, and dark rum, then ignited and served over ice cream. We're skipping the flames and boosting the banana flavor by serving this parfait-style over banana pudding and adding caramelized pecans for some crunch.

1 cup pecan halves

¼ cup maple syrup

1 (3.4-ounce) package vegan instant banana pudding mix

2 cups almond milk

⅓ cup vegan butter

¾ cup packed brown sugar

¼ teaspoon ground cinnamon

3 medium bananas, cut into rounds

1. Preheat the oven to 350°F. Line a small rimmed baking sheet with parchment paper.

2. In a small bowl, toss the pecans in the maple syrup. Spread out on the prepared baking sheet in an even layer and bake for 10 to 15 minutes, or until toasted and caramelized. Remove from the oven. Let cool completely, about 15 minutes.

3. Using an electric hand mixer in a medium bowl, beat the instant pudding mix and milk on medium for about 2 minutes, or until thickened. Refrigerate for about 30 minutes.

4. Meanwhile, in a wide skillet, melt the butter over medium-low heat. Stir in the sugar and cinnamon. Add the bananas and cook, stirring gently, for 3 to 5 minutes, or until glazed and softened.

5. Set out 4 parfait glasses and add a layer of pudding to each, followed by a layer of bananas and another layer of pudding. Coarsely chop the pecans and sprinkle on top of each parfait.

Variation tip: If you can't find instant banana pudding, use vanilla pudding and add 1 teaspoon banana extract to achieve the banana flavor.

Blackberry Eton Mess

PREP TIME: 25 minutes · **COOK TIME:** 1 hour 40 minutes
INACTIVE TIME: 1 hour 20 minutes

GLUTEN-FREE, NUT-FREE, SOY-FREE · SERVES: 6

Eton mess is a classic strawberry-based English dessert said to have originated in the late 1800s at Eton College. It's a delicious combination of crushed meringue cookies, fruit, and whipped cream. I use blackberries here because I think they're an underrated dessert berry and deserve a chance to shine!

FOR THE MERINGUE COOKIES
3 ounces aquafaba
2 teaspoons
  vanilla extract
½ teaspoon cream
  of tartar
¾ cup granulated sugar
3 tablespoons
  powdered sugar

**FOR THE
BLACKBERRY COMPOTE**
1 pint fresh
  blackberries, divided
½ cup granulated sugar
2 tablespoons fresh
  lemon juice

FOR THE TOPPING
1½ cups Coconut
  Whipped Cream
  (page 115) or
  store-bought
Fresh blackberries, for
  garnish (optional)

1. Preheat the oven to 200°F. Line 2 large rimmed baking sheets with parchment paper.

2. **Make the cookies:** Using an electric hand mixer in a large bowl, beat the aquafaba, vanilla, and cream of tartar on medium-high for 10 minutes, or until stiff peaks form. Slowly add the granulated sugar and powdered sugar and continue beating until the sugars have dissolved and the fluff is glossy.

3. Scoop tablespoons of the meringue onto the baking sheets, or use a piping bag fitted with a star tip and pipe out 18 (2-inch) meringues. Bake for 1 to 1½ hours, or until dry to the touch. Remove from the oven and let cool completely, about 1 hour.

4. **Make the blackberry compote:** In a wide saucepan, bring half the blackberries, the sugar, and lemon juice to a full boil, slightly mashing the berries as they cook. Reduce the heat and simmer for 10 minutes. Remove from the heat and fold in the remaining berries. Refrigerate for about 20 minutes, or until cold.

5. **To assemble:** Gently crush the meringues into big and small chunks. Divide evenly among 6 glasses or dishes. To each, add a layer of compote, another layer of meringues, and top with the whipped cream. Garnish with the berries (if using), and serve immediately or chill for 1 hour.

Raspberry-Chocolate Trifle

PREP TIME: 1 hour · **COOK TIME:** 35 minutes · **INACTIVE TIME:** 40 minutes

BIG BATCH, NUT-FREE · SERVES: 12

Trifles are as much fun to build as they are to eat. Typically consisting of a sponge cake layer, a fruit layer, and a custard layer, this dessert has many components—but don't let that frighten you. They're all easy to prepare, and you can make them ahead of time and keep them refrigerated until ready to assemble. I recommend using a trifle bowl for this dessert, but if you don't have one, any round, deep dish around 8 inches in diameter is fine.

FOR THE CAKE

5 tablespoons vegetable oil, plus more for greasing

1½ cups plus 3 tablespoons all-purpose flour

1 cup granulated sugar

1 teaspoon baking soda

½ teaspoon salt

1 cup water

2 teaspoons vanilla extract

1 teaspoon white vinegar

2 recipes Chocolate Mousse (page 83)

FOR THE RASPBERRY COULIS

1½ cups frozen raspberries

½ cup granulated sugar

3 tablespoons fresh orange juice

1. Preheat the oven to 350°F. Grease an 8-by-8-inch baking pan.

2. **Make the cake:** In a large bowl, combine the flour, sugar, baking soda, and salt. Add the water, oil, vanilla, and vinegar. Stir until no lumps remain. Pour into the prepared baking pan and bake for 35 minutes, or until a toothpick inserted in the center comes out clean. Remove from the oven. Let cool for 10 minutes, then refrigerate for about 30 minutes.

3. **Make the raspberry coulis:** Meanwhile, in a medium saucepan, cook the raspberries, sugar, and orange juice over medium heat for 4 to 6 minutes, or until the sugar dissolves and raspberries break down. Spoon into a fine-mesh sieve, straining to remove any seeds.

4. **Assemble the trifle:** Cut the cake in half horizontally to create 2 layers, then cut each layer into rectangles to fit in a trifle bowl. Place a layer of cake on the bottom of the trifle bowl, squishing pieces together as necessary to cover the bottom.

FOR THE TOPPINGS

2 pints fresh
  raspberries, divided

1 batch Coconut
  Whipped Cream
  (page 115)

2 tablespoons shaved
  dairy-free 70% dark
  chocolate

5. Add half of the mousse and spread evenly but don't pack it down. Add 1 pint of raspberries. Add the remaining cake to form 1 more layer. Add the coulis and top with the remaining mousse. Top with the whipped cream and garnish with the remaining pint of fresh raspberries and the shaved chocolate.

Lighten-up tip: An equal amount of applesauce can replace the sugar in the cake batter to keep it sweet and moist with less refined sugar. Decrease the amount of water to ¾ cup to keep your batter from becoming too thin.

6

NO-BAKE DESSERTS

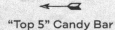

"Top 5" Candy Bar

Cinnamon and Maple Donut Holes

PREP TIME: 5 minutes · **INACTIVE TIME:** 25 minutes

GLUTEN-FREE, SOY-FREE · MAKES: 10 donut holes

These little bites are a great on-the-go snack. I like to coat them in a maple glaze, but they're just as good on their own or rolled in a mix of cinnamon and sugar. You can easily turn these into protein balls by adding vegan protein powder—look for a vanilla version to add extra vanilla flavor.

FOR THE DONUT HOLES

1 cup almond flour
¼ cup packed
   brown sugar
1½ teaspoons ground
   cinnamon
¼ teaspoon salt
⅛ teaspoon
   ground nutmeg
¼ cup solid coconut oil
1 tablespoon
   almond butter
1 tablespoon water
1 teaspoon vanilla extract

FOR THE GLAZE

2 cups powdered sugar
3 tablespoons
   unsweetened
   almond milk
2 tablespoons
   maple syrup

1. Line a large plate with parchment paper.

2. **Make the donut holes:** In a large bowl, combine the flour, sugar, cinnamon, salt, and nutmeg.

3. Using an electric hand mixer in a medium bowl, whisk or beat the oil, butter, water, and vanilla on medium until smooth.

4. Gradually add the dry ingredients and continue beating until a dough forms. Scoop tablespoons of dough into your hands and roll it into balls. Put the dough balls on the prepared plate and refrigerate for about 15 minutes.

5. **Make the glaze:** In a medium bowl, whisk the sugar, milk, and maple syrup until smooth and pourable but thick enough to coat the back of a spoon.

6. Using a fork, dip each donut hole into the glaze, then return them to the plate. Refrigerate for about 10 minutes to set the glaze.

Variation tip: Make these nut-free by swapping out the almond flour for coconut flour, the almond butter for tahini, and the almond milk for soy milk—or any another plant-based milk. Tahini is a great substitute for nut butters in any dish. Made from ground sesame seeds, tahini adds a wonderful nutty flavor without actually containing any nuts. Be sure to stir tahini really well before using. Just like with all-natural nut butters, the oil separates when it sits.

Lemony Coconut Snowballs

PREP TIME: 5 minutes · **INACTIVE TIME:** 30 minutes

BIG BATCH, GLUTEN-FREE, SOY-FREE · **MAKES:** 12 to 16 balls

Lemon lovers take note! These little bites are full of tart lemon flavor balanced out by deliciously sweet coconut and maple syrup. They're also one of the easiest recipes in this book—just mix everything in a food processor, roll the dough into little balls, chill, and eat. Don't worry—if you don't have access to a food processor, just swap out the raw almonds for the same amount of almond flour and mix by hand.

2½ cups shredded
   unsweetened
   coconut, divided
½ cup raw almonds
3 tablespoons fresh
   lemon juice
2 tablespoons
   maple syrup
2 tablespoons coconut
   oil, melted
1 tablespoon lemon zest

1. Line a plate with parchment paper. Put ½ cup of shredded coconut in a shallow bowl.

2. In a food processor, process the remaining 2 cups of shredded coconut, the almonds, lemon juice, maple syrup, oil, and zest until a dough forms.

3. Scoop out tablespoons of dough. Using clean hands, roll them into balls. Toss one ball at a time in the reserved coconut and then transfer to the prepared plate. Refrigerate for at least 30 minutes before eating. Refrigerate leftovers in an airtight container for 2 to 3 days.

Peppermint Candy Cane Bark

PREP TIME: 25 minutes · **INACTIVE TIME:** 45 minutes

BIG BATCH, GLUTEN-FREE, KID-FRIENDLY, NUT-FREE, SOY-FREE
MAKES: about 2 pounds

Peppermint bark is a classic holiday treat. I make pounds of it each year for family and friends and it takes until St. Patrick's Day to get the peppermint smell out of my kitchen! For the dairy-free white chocolate layer, I use kosher white chocolate chips, which are easy to find online or at kosher grocery stores. Kosher dietary laws restrict the mixing of meat and milk products so many kosher products are made *pareve*, which means they contain neither dairy nor meat-based ingredients, making them great for vegan baking.

2 cups dairy-free dark chocolate chips

1 teaspoon peppermint extract

3 candy canes or 8 to 10 peppermint candies, finely crushed, divided

2½ cups dairy-free white chocolate chips

1. Line a 9-by-13-inch baking pan or rimmed baking sheet with wax paper.

2. In a heat-proof glass bowl set over a pot filled with 2 to 3 inches of simmering water, heat the dark chocolate, stirring constantly, until melted.

3. While still stirring, add the peppermint extract, then remove from the heat and very quickly pour the chocolate onto the prepared pan, smoothing out to evenly cover the whole dish. Sprinkle with half of the crushed candy canes, then freeze for 15 minutes.

4. Once chilled, repeat step 2 to melt the white chocolate chips, stirring constantly, until smooth.

5. Pour the white chocolate evenly over the frozen chocolate layer and top with the remaining candy canes. Freeze for 30 minutes, or until solid. Break into pieces and store in the refrigerator in an airtight container for up to 2 weeks.

Variation tip: For an autumnal treat, swap out the peppermint extract and candy canes for 1 tablespoon orange zest and 1 cup each chopped roasted almonds and dried cranberries.

Peanut Butter Cups with Sea Salt

PREP TIME: 15 minutes · **INACTIVE TIME:** 2 hours 15 minutes

GLUTEN-FREE, KID-FRIENDLY, SOY-FREE · MAKES: 12 peanut butter cups

This dessert is so simple I guarantee you'll have it on repeat. It uses only five ingredients and takes just a few minutes to assemble—the hardest part of this dessert is waiting for it to set up! Rich chocolate surrounds a creamy, sweet peanut butter filling that has just a hint of added sea salt. To shake this up a bit, try using crunchy peanut butter or add chopped dry-roasted peanuts.

2 cups dairy-free chocolate chips, divided

2 teaspoons coconut oil, divided

1 cup creamy peanut butter

½ cup powdered sugar

½ teaspoon sea salt, divided

1. Line a standard muffin tin with liners.

2. In a heat-proof glass bowl set over a pot filled with 2 to 3 inches of simmering water, heat 1 cup of chocolate chips and 1 teaspoon of oil, stirring frequently, until melted. (Or heat in the microwave in 30-second intervals until melted and combined, stirring in between.)

3. Divide the chocolate evenly among the prepared muffin cups. Refrigerate for 15 minutes.

4. Meanwhile, using an electric hand mixer in a medium bowl, beat the peanut butter, sugar, and ¼ teaspoon of salt on medium until fully combined. Divide the filling evenly among each chocolate cup. Return the tin to the refrigerator.

5. Repeat step 2 to melt the remaining 1 cup of chocolate chips and 1 teaspoon of oil.

6. Pour the chocolate over the peanut butter layer and sprinkle with the remaining ¼ teaspoon of salt. Refrigerate for about 2 hours, or until firm. Store in an airtight container in the refrigerator for up to 1 week.

Variation tip: Use a mini muffin tin to make mini peanut butter cups.

Chocolate, Cherry, and Almond Truffles

PREP TIME: 1 hour · **INACTIVE TIME:** 4 hours

BIG BATCH, GLUTEN-FREE, SOY-FREE · MAKES: about 40 truffles

My grandfather loved the flavor combination of cherry and chocolate. His favorites were chocolate-cherry cordials. (The man could eat an entire box of Russell Stover cordials in the blink of an eye.) I'm not a huge fan of maraschino cherries, but I do love a good cream-centered truffle, so I made these fondant truffles to pay homage to him. Traditional fondant cream uses powdered sugar only, but I added almond flour and almond extract partially because almond and cherry go so well together, and because they help thicken the filling into a cross between fondant and marzipan.

¼ cup frozen cherries, thawed

¼ cup vegan butter, at room temperature

3 tablespoons corn syrup

¼ teaspoon salt

3 cups powdered sugar, divided

½ cup almond flour

½ teaspoon vanilla extract

½ teaspoon almond extract

1 to 2 drops vegan red gel food coloring

2¾ cups dairy-free chocolate chips

1 tablespoon coconut oil

1. In a small bowl, mash the cherries with a fork until mostly pureed. Drain in a small fine-mesh sieve to remove excess liquid.

2. Using an electric hand mixer in a large bowl, beat the butter, corn syrup, and salt on medium for about 3 minutes, or until smooth. Add ½ cup of sugar and the flour. Beat until incorporated. In ½-cup increments, add 1½ cups of sugar, beating until fully incorporated in between additions.

3. Add the cherry puree, vanilla, almond extract, and food coloring. Mix until solid pink. Add ½ cup of sugar and beat on medium until incorporated. If the filling is thick enough to scoop, refrigerate for 1 hour. If it's still loose, add the remaining ½ cup of sugar, 2 tablespoons at a time, until the desired thickness is reached, then refrigerate for 1 hour.

4. Line a large rimmed baking sheet (or 2 small ones) with parchment paper. Working quickly so your hands don't heat up the fondant too much, scoop a tablespoon of fondant into your hand and roll it into a ball. Place on the prepared baking sheet. Repeat with the remaining fondant. Put the baking sheet in the freezer to set while you make the chocolate coating.

5. In a heat-proof glass bowl set over a pot filled with 2 to 3 inches of simmering water, heat the chocolate chips and oil, stirring frequently, until melted. Remove from the heat.

6. Using a fork, lower the fondant balls one at a time into the chocolate, letting the excess drip off before placing the truffles back onto the baking sheet. Refrigerate for 3 hours. For best results, keep refrigerated for up to 2 weeks or frozen for up to 2 months.

Variation tip: If you're not a fan of almond or are allergic to nuts, replace the almond flour with an equal amount of powdered sugar and skip the almond extract.

Cookies and Caramel Candy Bars

PREP TIME: 40 minutes · **INACTIVE TIME:** 1 hour

KID-FRIENDLY, SOY-FREE · MAKES: 12 bars

This is an easy, no-bake copycat version of a classic candy bar—you know, the one with the salty-sweet shortbread-style cookie topped with creamy caramel and wrapped in a coating of luscious chocolate? Yeah, that one. This recipe uses Medjool dates to form the base of the caramel layer, which not only eliminates the need for added refined sugar, but also doesn't require a pot, stovetop, or a candy thermometer (plus it's super sweet and delicious). A win-win situation for sure! Since this is a no-bake recipe, I recommend keeping these bars in the refrigerator or freezer until serving to help them keep their shape.

FOR THE COOKIE BASE
2 cups rolled oats
1 cup almond flour
3 tablespoons
  agave nectar
3 tablespoons coconut
  oil, melted
½ teaspoon salt

FOR THE CARAMEL LAYER
9 pitted Medjool dates,
  softened
¼ cup hot water
2 tablespoons
  cashew butter
2 tablespoons coconut
  oil, melted

1. Line a 4½-by-8½-inch standard loaf pan on all 4 sides with plastic wrap or parchment paper.

2. **Make the cookie base:** In a food processor, grind the oats into a fine powder. In a large mixing bowl, combine the oats, flour, agave, oil, and salt. Using a spatula, mix until the base sticks together when pressed between your fingers (like wet sand). Press firmly into the pre-pared pan to form a crust. Refrigerate while you prepare the caramel layer.

3. **Make the caramel layer:** In a food processor or blender, puree the dates, water, butter, and oil until thick and smooth. Pour the caramel over the cookie base, spreading with a spatula to ensure complete coverage. Refrigerate for about 45 minutes, or until firm.

4. Line a rimmed baking sheet with parchment paper and place a wire rack on top. Cut the chilled bar into 12 slices.

**FOR THE
CHOCOLATE COATING**

1 cup dairy-free
  chocolate chips
1 tablespoon coconut oil

5. **Make the chocolate coating:** In a heat-proof glass bowl set over a pot filled with 2 to 3 inches of simmering water, heat the chocolate chips and oil, stirring frequently, until melted. (Or heat in the microwave in 30-second intervals until melted, stirring in between.) Pour into a wide, shallow bowl.

6. Using a fork, dip each bar into the chocolate and place on the rack to allow the excess to drip. Once the chocolate has set and no longer looks glossy or wet, about 15 minutes, transfer to an airtight container and refrigerate until serving.

Make-ahead tip: You can refrigerate these candy bars for up to 2 weeks or freeze them in a resealable freezer bag for up to 3 months. If frozen, thaw them at room temperature for 10 to 15 minutes before eating.

"Top 5" Candy Bar

PREP TIME: 35 minutes · INACTIVE TIME: 2 hours 20 minutes

BIG BATCH, SOY-FREE · MAKES: 24 bars

I call this a "Top 5" bar because it has five of my all-time favorite ingredients in it: chocolate, caramel, peanuts, coconut, and pretzels, combined in a chewy, salty, sweet little package perfect for sharing. Because this recipe is no-bake, it's pretty simple to make; it just takes time to chill. I definitely recommend keeping these treats in the refrigerator to help keep their chewy, firm texture.

FOR THE BASE

2 cups salted
   pretzel sticks
1½ cups creamy peanut
   butter, divided
¾ cup vegan
   butter, melted
1 cup powdered sugar

FOR THE CARAMEL

2 cups pitted Medjool
   dates, softened
1 cup unsweetened
   almond milk
1 teaspoon vanilla extract
¼ teaspoon salt

FOR THE TOPPING

2 cups
   dry-roasted peanuts
¾ cup shredded
   unsweetened coconut
2½ cups dairy-free
   chocolate chips
2 tablespoons
   coconut oil

1. Line a 9-by-13-inch baking pan with parchment paper.

2. **Make the base:** In a food processor, crush the pretzel sticks into crumbs. (Or you can place them in a resealable bag and crush with a rolling pin.)

3. Transfer to a large bowl. Add 1 cup of peanut butter, the butter, and sugar. Stir until the mixture comes together like a dough. Press firmly into the bottom of the prepared baking pan and refrigerate while you make the next layer.

4. **Make the caramel:** In a food processor or in a high-speed blender, pulse the dates, milk, vanilla, and salt until smooth. Pour on top of the base, spreading with a spatula to cover evenly. Refrigerate for 30 minutes.

5. Melt the remaining ½ cup of peanut butter in the microwave for about 30 seconds, or until pourable. Pour evenly over the caramel layer, then top with the peanuts and shredded coconut. Refrigerate for 1 hour.

6. Line a rimmed baking sheet with parchment paper. Cut the bar into 2-inch squares. Place on the prepared baking sheet and freeze for about 20 minutes.

7. In a heat-proof glass bowl set over a pot filled with 2 to 3 inches of simmering water, heat the chocolate chips and oil, stirring frequently, until melted.

8. Using a fork, coat the squares one at a time in the chocolate. Return to the baking sheet and refrigerate for 20 to 30 minutes.

Make-ahead tip: You can refrigerate these candy bars for up to 2 weeks or freeze them in a resealable freezer bag for up to 3 months. If frozen, thaw them at room temperature for 10 to 15 minutes before eating.

Chocolate Lasagna

PREP TIME: 40 minutes · **INACTIVE TIME:** 3 hours 45 minutes

BIG BATCH, KID-FRIENDLY, NUT-FREE, SOY-FREE · SERVES: 16

Who says lasagna can't be served for dessert? Definitely not me. While the amount of prep might be intimidating, it's a very simple layered dessert that requires just a little bit of mixing time and lots of chill time to set up. I guarantee when you slice and serve it, your guests will think you're a hero! I used both vanilla and chocolate for the pudding layer, but feel free to experiment. This recipe uses "coconut beverage," which is sold in cartons, as opposed to cans.

FOR THE CRUST

1 tablespoon vegan butter, at room temperature, plus 6 tablespoons melted

1 (10-ounce) package vegan chocolate sandwich cookies, crushed

¼ teaspoon salt

FOR THE CREAM CHEESE LAYER

1 (8-ounce) package vegan cream cheese, at room temperature

¼ cup granulated sugar

2 tablespoons coconut milk

½ teaspoon vanilla extract

1½ cups Coconut Whipped Cream (page 115) or store-bought

1. **Make the crust:** Grease a 9-by-13-inch baking pan with the room temperature butter. In a large bowl, mix the crushed cookies, melted butter, and salt until well combined. Pour the mixture into the prepared baking pan and press down firmly to cover the bottom to form a crust. Freeze for about 15 minutes.

2. **Make the cream cheese layer:** Meanwhile, using an electric hand mixer, in a large bowl, beat the cream cheese, sugar, coconut milk, and vanilla on medium until thoroughly combined. Fold or gently mix in the whipped cream, then pour the entire mixture over the crust, spreading evenly with an offset spatula or the back of a spoon. Freeze for another 15 minutes.

FOR THE PUDDING LAYER

1 (3.4-ounce) package
vegan instant
chocolate pudding mix

1 (3.4-ounce) package
vegan instant vanilla
pudding mix

4 cups coconut milk
beverage

3 cups Coconut Whipped
Cream (page 115)
or store-bought,
for topping

2 cups dairy-free
chocolate chips, for
decorating

3. **Make the pudding layer:** Meanwhile, using an electric hand mixer in another large bowl, beat or whisk the chocolate pudding mix, vanilla pudding mix, and coconut beverage on medium for about 3 minutes, or until slightly thickened and smooth. Pour over the cream cheese layer and freeze for about another 15 minutes.

4. Spread the whipped cream on top. Sprinkle with the chocolate chips. Cover loosely with plastic wrap and refrigerate for about 3 hours.

Lighten-up tip: Use an unsweetened coconut milk beverage in this recipe to avoid adding extra sugar.

Make-ahead tip: This dish can sit in the refrigerator for up to 3 days before being sliced, so if you're making it for a special occasion, consider prepping it a day or two ahead of time.

Over-the-Top Rice Cereal Treats

PREP TIME: 10 minutes · **COOK TIME:** 5 minutes · **INACTIVE TIME:** 30 minutes

BIG BATCH, SOY-FREE · MAKES: 12 to 16 squares

Okay, so you can share these with your kids if you want to . . . but it's perfectly okay to keep them for yourself. Rather than use marshmallow as the base, these rice cereal squares use a sweet, sticky syrup made from maple syrup and melted peanut butter. The chopped pecans and shredded coconut add great texture to these treats too. If you don't have chopped pecans, you could use roasted peanuts or simply choose a crunchy peanut butter instead. I like using brown rice crisp cereals because they add a nuttier flavor, but white rice crisp cereals work just as well.

1½ cups unflavored rice crisp cereal

1½ cups chocolate rice crisp cereal

⅓ cup chopped pecans

⅓ cup shredded unsweetened coconut

⅓ cup creamy peanut butter

⅓ cup maple syrup

½ teaspoon vanilla extract

½ teaspoon almond extract

1. Line an 8-by-8-inch baking pan with parchment paper, leaving some extra hanging over all sides.

2. In a large bowl, combine the unflavored rice crisp cereal, chocolate rice crisp cereal, pecans, and coconut.

3. In a small saucepan over medium heat, cook the peanut butter, maple syrup, vanilla, and almond extract, stirring, for about 5 minutes, or until melted and bubbly. Pour into the bowl with the dry ingredients and stir vigorously until fully incorporated.

4. Transfer the mixture to the prepared baking pan and press down firmly into a tightly packed, even layer. Freeze for 30 minutes, then cut into squares.

SWEET STAPLES

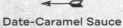

Date-Caramel Sauce

No-Fail Piecrust

PREP TIME: 10 minutes · **INACTIVE TIME:** 30 minutes

NUT-FREE, SOY-FREE · MAKES: 1 (9-inch) crust

This is a classic piecrust that works for both sweet and savory dishes. You'll find it handy for various recipes in this book, such as Grandma's Blueberry Pie (page 71) and Mile-High Lemon Meringue Pie (page 70). This recipe makes a single 9-inch crust, so for a pie that requires both top and bottom crusts, simply double this recipe. For best results, chill the vegan butter in the freezer for 15 to 30 minutes before making this crust.

1½ cups all-purpose flour
½ teaspoon salt
½ cup vegan butter, cold
4 to 5 tablespoons
   cold water

1. In a large bowl, combine the flour and salt. Add the butter and, using a pastry cutter, cut the butter into the flour until it resembles coarse cornmeal, meaning that there are no large visible chunks of butter. (If you don't have a pastry cutter, use 2 knives, cutting in criss-cross motions.)

2. Add the water, 2 tablespoons at a time, and using your hands, work the dough together. Add more water, 1 tablespoon at a time, until the dough comes together in a ball.

3. Turn out the dough onto plastic wrap and form into a disc. Tightly wrap the dough and refrigerate for about 30 minutes to firm up before rolling out.

Make ahead tip: The wrapped, uncooked dough will last up to 24 hours in the refrigerator. The dough will be quite stiff, so allow it to rest on the counter for 15 minutes before rolling out.

Eggless Meringue

PREP TIME: 30 minutes · **INACTIVE TIME:** 20 minutes

GLUTEN-FREE, NUT-FREE, ONE-BOWL, SOY-FREE · MAKES: about 2 cups

This recipe is an absolute game-changer for vegan baking. All those desserts you thought had to be avoided because they couldn't be made vegan are back—and better than ever! This recipe is perfect for my Mile-High Lemon Meringue Pie (page 70). You can also use this recipe to make meringue cookies, pavlovas, or any other egg white–based dessert! Like regular egg whites, aquafaba meringue can be finicky and takes time, but your electric mixer does all the work here for you.

3 ounces aquafaba

½ teaspoon cream of tartar

¾ cup granulated sugar

½ teaspoon vanilla extract (optional)

1. Chill a metal bowl (or the bowl of a stand mixer) in the freezer for 15 to 20 minutes, then wipe dry.

2. Using an electric hand mixer in the bowl or a stand mixer fitted with whisk attachment, beat the aquafaba and cream of tartar on medium-high for at least 6 minutes, or until soft peaks form.

3. Continue beating and gradually add the sugar, 1 tablespoon at a time for 15 to 20 minutes, or until stiff peaks form and the meringue has a glossy shine to it. Add the vanilla (if using) and beat for 1 to 2 minutes.

Dark Chocolate Ganache

PREP TIME: 10 minutes

GLUTEN-FREE, NUT-FREE, SOY-FREE · MAKES: 1½ cups

Unlike frosting, which is made from butter and powdered sugar and is super sweet, ganache is a rich, silky chocolate topping that can be used as a filling, dip, spread, or frosting. It's made from two ingredients only: high-quality, semisweet chocolate and heavy cream. For this recipe I recommend using coconut cream, since it's the thickest of all plant-based creams, but if you can find heavy soy cream (and you're okay with soy), that will work too. You can use this dark chocolate ganache as a filling for any of the cakes in this book. Or use it as a frosting: simply let it cool at room temperature for 2 hours, then whip with a whisk (or an electric mixer) until light and fluffy.

1 (8-ounce) package dairy-free semisweet chocolate, chopped

1 cup coconut cream

1. Put the chocolate in a medium bowl.
2. In a saucepan, bring the cream to a simmer over medium heat. Pour over the chocolate and let sit for 2 to 3 minutes, then stir to combine. Let cool slightly, then pour over a cake.

Lighten-up tip: This recipe uses semisweet chocolate, which is about 50% sugar. Ganache often tops recipes that already contain a fair amount of sugar, so try making this recipe with dairy-free dark chocolate (70% cocoa) to reduce the sugar content. Coconut cream is naturally sweet, so your ganache will be sweet too.

Make-ahead tip: Ganache will keep in the refrigerator for up to 5 days in an airtight container.

Dairy-Free Buttercream Frosting

PREP TIME: 10 minutes

BIG BATCH, GLUTEN-FREE, KID-FRIENDLY, ONE-BOWL, NUT-FREE, SOY-FREE
MAKES: 8 cups

This is one of my most-requested recipes (along with a basic vanilla cupcake). This frosting is luscious and creamy and virtually identical to its dairy-laden counterpart. The trick to making this icing smooth and spreadable is room-temperature vegan butter. The softer the butter, the more easily it will blend with the powdered sugar. If the butter is too cold, it won't blend and will leave you with lumpy buttercream. This yield is enough for a 12-inch two-layer cake or two to four dozen cupcakes, depending on the amount used per cupcake. This recipe works well on the Snickerdoodle Cupcakes with Brown Sugar Buttercream (page 40) and Cookies and Cream Cupcakes (page 46) and is a great substitute for the chocolate glaze on my Dreamy Cream-Filled Chocolate Cupcakes (page 42).

2 cups vegan butter, at room temperature
6 cups powdered sugar
1 teaspoon vanilla extract
Pinch salt

Using an electric hand mixer in a large bowl, beat the butter on medium-high until pale and creamy. Reduce the speed to medium. Add the sugar, ½ cup at a time, mixing well, for about 5 minutes. Add the vanilla and salt. Increase the speed to medium-high and beat for about 1 minute, or until smooth.

Variation tip: Swap 1 cup powdered sugar for 1 cup cocoa powder and mix on low until smooth for glorious chocolate buttercream. To make colored buttercream, use vegan gel food coloring and mix in by hand after the frosting is fully mixed. I recommend Wilton brand gel food coloring because it's not made with any animal by-products.

Apple Pie Filling

PREP TIME: 10 minutes · **COOK TIME:** 15 minutes · **INACTIVE TIME:** 1 hour

GLUTEN-FREE, NUT-FREE, SOY-FREE · MAKES: about 4 cups

I love this apple pie filling. It's reminiscent of a caramel apple, thanks to the brown sugar and butter in the sauce, and is a delicious treat on top of ice cream, in a pie, on top of a coffee cake—or just eaten straight out of the jar! This filling freezes well too, so you can keep a batch on hand and defrost it overnight in the refrigerator before using. I prefer Granny Smith apples because of their tart flavor and stiff structure, but you could use Honeycrisp or other tart red apples. Try this pie filling in my Ginger-Pear Pie Bites (page 65) or as a great autumnal take on Grandma's Blueberry Pie (page 71).

6 medium Granny Smith apples, peeled and finely diced (about 4 cups)

2 tablespoons fresh lemon juice

½ cup granulated sugar

½ cup packed brown sugar

¼ cup cornstarch

1 teaspoon ground cinnamon

¼ teaspoon ground nutmeg

2 cups water

1 cup apple juice

1 tablespoon vegan butter, at room temperature

1. In a large bowl, combine the apples and lemon juice.

2. In another bowl, combine the granulated sugar, brown sugar, cornstarch, cinnamon, and nutmeg. Add the water and apple juice. Whisk to combine. Pour the mixture into a wide saucepan and bring to a boil. Reduce the heat to medium, add the apples, and cook for about 10 minutes, or until the apples are soft and the sauce has thickened.

3. Remove from the heat and add the butter, stirring until incorporated. Let it cool at room temperature for about 1 hour, or until completely cooled. Transfer to an airtight container and refrigerate for up to 3 days or freeze for up to 3 months.

Lighten-up tip: Use an unsweetened or no-sugar-added apple juice to avoid extra sugar. You can also reduce the amount of granulated sugar to taste—or omit it altogether.

Date-Caramel Sauce

PREP TIME: 5 minutes

GLUTEN-FREE, NUT-FREE, ONE-BOWL, SOY-FREE · MAKES: 1½ cups

I pair this date sauce with everything—literally everything. It's a fantastic dip for sliced fruit and a great sundae topping, and it works well as a filling or topping for cakes and pies. This sauce is a great addition to my Triple Pudding Parfait (page 81) or drizzled over my Chocolate and Coconut Dream Bars (page 34). It's rich and delicious just like this, but if you want to give it a grown-up flavor boost, add a tablespoon of dark rum when blending—just keep it away from the kids!

2 cups pitted Medjool dates, softened
¾ cup coconut milk
½ cup maple syrup
1 teaspoon vanilla extract
¼ teaspoon salt

In a high-speed blender or food processor, blend the dates, milk, maple syrup, vanilla, and salt until smooth and creamy. Refrigerate in an airtight container for 2 to 3 weeks.

Ingredient tip: If your dates are a little too firm or dry, as many packaged grocery-store dates tend to be, soak them in hot water for 30 minutes before adding to this recipe. The hot water will reconstitute them, adding moisture and softness back.

Vanilla Custard

PREP TIME: 5 minutes · **COOK TIME:** 10 minutes · **INACTIVE TIME:** 30 minutes

GLUTEN-FREE, ONE-BOWL, SOY-FREE · MAKES: about 2 cups

This recipe is a definite sweet staple, and I predict it will quickly become one of your favorites. It only takes a few minutes to make and is incredibly versatile. It's the perfect filling for my Strawberry Custard Napoleons (page 73), and it's fantastic as a filling for my Raspberry-Chocolate Trifle (page 88) or as a pudding topped with fresh fruit.

1 cup cashew milk

1 cup full-fat
  coconut milk

½ cup maple syrup

¼ cup cornstarch

1 tablespoon
  vanilla extract

⅛ teaspoon ground
  turmeric

In a medium saucepan, simmer the cashew milk, coconut milk, maple syrup, cornstarch, and vanilla, whisking constantly, for 5 to 10 minutes, or until thickened. Remove from the heat and whisk in the turmeric. Let cool completely.

Variation tip: Vanilla is a classic custard flavor, but you can also switch this up by swapping out the vanilla extract for almond extract. I'd recommend using half the amount of extract to start, since it has a very strong flavor and can make a dish taste like perfume if you use too much.

Coconut Whipped Cream

PREP TIME: 10 minutes · **INACTIVE TIME:** 12 hours

GLUTEN-FREE, NUT-FREE, ONE-BOWL, SOY-FREE · MAKES: about 1½ cups

Whipped cream makes everything better, and now you can make your own dairy-free whipped cream at home. You'll need either an electric mixer or a stand mixer with a whisk attachment. I don't recommend trying it by hand because it needs consistent speed and intensity to whip it. The trick to getting this whipped cream to work is refrigerating the can of coconut cream for long enough to allow the cream to separate and rise to the top. We do this because the cream is the part that will whip, whereas the water won't, so refrigerating it allows that part to naturally separate.

1 (13.5-ounce) can coconut cream, refrigerated overnight
2 tablespoons sugar
1 teaspoon vanilla extract

1. Carefully open and scoop out the cream part from the top of the can, making sure not to shake the can in any way. (You can save the water for another use—like a smoothie.) Transfer to a bowl.

2. Using an electric hand mixer, beat the coconut cream on medium for about 2 minutes, then increase the speed to high and beat for 5 to 6 minutes, or until stiff peaks form. Add the sugar and vanilla and beat for 1 minute. Refrigerate until needed.

Technique tip: Since separating the cream from the coconut water is a long process, get in the habit of keeping one or two cans of coconut cream in your refrigerator all the time. That way, when you need one for baking, it's ready to go. Keep it in the middle or front of your refrigerator where it's less cold. If you store it at the back long term, it's likely to freeze!

Ingredient tip: Not all coconut cream is created equal, and some work better in sauces and soups, while others are more suited to desserts. We all have our favorites, and these are the brands I recommend most for consistent results when making whipped cream: Aroy-D, Native Forest, Thai Kitchen, and Savoy. These national brands are typically available at almost all grocery stores.

Desserts by Occasion

BAKE SALES OR POTLUCKS

Soft and Chewy Lemon and
  Poppy Seed Cookies **18**
Blueberry Cheesecake Bars **32**
Lemon Squares **33**
Coconut Cream Mini Tarts **64**
Canadian Butter Tarts **66**

KIDS' PARTIES

Bakery-Style Sprinkle Cookies **20**
New York–Style Black and
  White Cookies **22**
Cookies and Cream Cupcakes **46**
Ice Cream Sundae Cupcake Cones **44**
Strawberry-Vanilla Baked
  D'oh-nuts **47**

FALL AND WINTER HOLIDAYS

Cinnamon-Pecan Swirls **26**
Apple Pie Cookies **31**
Carrot Cake with
  Cream Cheese Frosting **52**
Peppermint Candy Cane Bark **94**
Frozen Chocolate-Peppermint
  Mousse Pots **79**

WEDDING OR BABY SHOWERS

Bakery-Style Sprinkle Cookies **20**
New York–Style Black and
  White Cookies **22**
Lemon Squares **33**
Chocolate Éclair Bars **36**
Italian Rainbow Cookies **29**
Toasted Coconut Layer Cake **56**

SPRING AND SUMMER DESSERTS

Easy Summer Peach and
  Berry Cobbler **68**
Mile-High Lemon Meringue Pie **70**
Grandma's Blueberry Pie **71**
Strawberry Custard Napoleons **73**
Rainbow Sherbet **78**

SPECIAL OCCASIONS

Blackberry Eton Mess **87**
Black Forest Cake **58**
Raspberry-Chocolate Trifle **88**
Toasted Coconut Layer Cake **56**
Mini Dark Chocolate and
  Caramel Tarts **69**

Measurement Conversions

VOLUME EQUIVALENTS	U.S. STANDARD	U.S. STANDARD (OUNCES)	METRIC (APPROXIMATE)
LIQUID	2 tablespoons	1 fl. oz.	30 mL
	¼ cup	2 fl. oz.	60 mL
	½ cup	4 fl. oz.	120 mL
	1 cup	8 fl. oz.	240 mL
	1½ cups	12 fl. oz.	355 mL
	2 cups or 1 pint	16 fl. oz.	475 mL
	4 cups or 1 quart	32 fl. oz.	1 L
	1 gallon	128 fl. oz.	4 L
DRY	⅛ teaspoon		0.5 mL
	¼ teaspoon		1 mL
	½ teaspoon		2 mL
	¾ teaspoon		4 mL
	1 teaspoon		5 mL
	1 tablespoon		15 mL
	¼ cup		59 mL
	⅓ cup		79 mL
	½ cup		118 mL
	⅔ cup		156 mL
	¾ cup		177 mL
	1 cup		235 mL
	2 cups or 1 pint		475 mL
	3 cups		700 mL
	4 cups or 1 quart		1 L
	½ gallon		2 L
	1 gallon		4 L

OVEN TEMPERATURES

FAHRENHEIT	CELSIUS (APPROXIMATE)
250°F	120°C
300°F	150°C
325°F	165°C
350°F	180°C
375°F	190°C
400°F	200°C
425°F	220°C
450°F	230°C

WEIGHT EQUIVALENTS

U.S. STANDARD	METRIC (APPROXIMATE)
½ ounce	15 g
1 ounce	30 g
2 ounces	60 g
4 ounces	115 g
8 ounces	225 g
12 ounces	340 g
16 ounces or 1 pound	455 g

Index

C

Acknowledgments

It's an incredible journey to bring a book to life, and it takes an amazing group of people to turn an idea into a full-fledged book. I'm so grateful to the entire team at Callisto Media for working so hard to help me create this book for you.

My most heartfelt thanks to Vanessa Putt for giving me the opportunity to write this book and to Gleni Bartels, my editor, for making this process so easy for me. Thank you for all your guidance, hard work, and enthusiasm for this book.

To my developmental editor, Sasha Tropp, thank you for ensuring this book "works" and for making my recipes come alive. To the entire production, art, and marketing teams assigned to this project—thank you for all your hard work to build and promote this book. Your efforts are truly appreciated.

About the Author

 **ALLY LAZARE** is a Toronto-based food blogger, writer, and home cook. She is the author of *Ally's Kitchen: Comfort Food—100 Easy, Plant-Based Meals for Everyone* and *The Budget-Friendly Vegan Cookbook: Healthy Meals for a Plant-Based Diet*.

Ally found her love of cooking and baking as a teenager and has been creating recipes ever since. When she and her family adopted a plant-based lifestyle almost 10 years ago, Ally focused on transforming all her signature dishes into plant-based delights and sharing her culinary knowledge with others through her blog and on social media.

When she's not cooking, Ally is busy collecting vintage cookbooks and spending time with her husband and two young daughters. You can follow Ally's culinary journeys on Instagram at @allylazare.

CPSIA information can be obtained
at www.ICGtesting.com
Printed in the USA
BVHW051802111120
592865BV00017B/18